CAN'T WON'T
COOK COOK

CAN'T WON'T COOK COOK

AINSLEY HARRIOTT

Photos by Juliet Piddington

BBC BOOKS

This book is published to accompany the television series entitled
Can't Cook Won't Cook which was first broadcast in 1995.
The series is produced by Bazal Productions for BBC Birmingham.
Executive Producer: Linda Clifford
Producer: Caroline Officer

Published by BBC Books,
an imprint of BBC Worldwide Publishing,
BBC Worldwide Ltd, Woodlands,
80 Wood Lane, London W12 0TT

First published 1997
Format © Bazal Productions
© Ainsley Harriott 1997
Recipes written by Orla Broderick and Susie Magasiner
The moral right of the author has been asserted.

ISBN 0 563 38323 2

Designed by Design/Section, Frome
Photographs by Juliet Piddington
Home Economist: Sarah Ramsbottom

Set in Gill Sans, News Gothic and 55 Helvetica Roman
Printed in Great Britain by Martins the Printers Ltd, Berwick-upon-Tweed
Bound in Great Britain by Hunter & Foulis Ltd, Edinburgh
Colour separation by Radstock Reproductions Ltd, Midsomer Norton
Cover printed by Clays Ltd, St Ives plc

Contents

Introduction 7

Before You Start 8

Basic Cooking Techniques 8

About the Recipes 10

Basic Cooking Equipment 11

Vegetarian Dishes 12

Fish Dishes 21

Poultry Dishes 36

Meat Dishes 56

Desserts 76

Index 95

Introduction

First, a very warm welcome to the *Can't Cook Won't Cook* cookbook. It's strange how many people feel alienated when it comes to cooking, and yet there's no need to panic. Being in the kitchen for the first time is rather like learning to drive a car. You have to practise using the equipment and work your way round the controls and then, when you've got used to it, the world's your oyster.

The idea behind the series, and the book, is to show how easy it is to cook good food, even if you're a novice. The simple step-by-step methods from the programmes have been used in the book, so you can see at a glance how straightforward these recipes are. Talking of glances I believe presentation is part of the success of a dish, so I have included quick tips on how to make fun garnishes like radish flowers and spring onion lotuses. Of course, if you're pressed for time, leave these out. Either way you'll not only end up with superb tasty dishes, but you'll find your confidence in the kitchen growing. Most importantly of all, I hope the book will get you cooking.

I always stress the fun element of cooking – it's so important. In my home the kitchen is the heart of the house, just as it was when I was growing up. I used to help my mum mix, beat, rub and sing our way round the table, cooker and chairs – it's funny how some things don't change! Perhaps the only difference today is that we want things in a hurry, especially when it comes to meals. Now you can call upon *Can't Cook Won't Cook* for a range of meal ideas, anything from a simple gourmet dish to a light delicious supper or mouthwatering dessert. Go on, rattle those pots and pans, then get ready to tickle those tastebuds!

Happy, smelly cooking to you all.

Before You Start

Read the recipe carefully before you start to make a dish so that you understand it totally. Then collect together the cooking equipment and all the ingredients you will need. Finally, weigh and measure out the ingredients. If you are a new cook, follow the recipe precisely to begin with, using the exact quantities and ingredients. When it comes to seasonings, herbs, flavourings, spices and sweetenings, however, they can usually be varied to suit individual tastes.

Basic Cooking Techniques

This alphabetical list is for you to refer to when you need a more detailed explanation of what to do when following a recipe.

BEAT To agitate an ingredient or mixture, using a wooden spoon, fork or whisk, to incorporate air and to make it smooth.

BLANCH To immerse food briefly in boiling water to remove its skin, whiten it or destroy enzymes and preserve its colour, flavour and texture, ready for freezing.

BLEND To mix foods together evenly using a spoon, food processor or electric blender.

BOIL To cook in a liquid, such as water, stock or milk, at a minimum temperature of 100°C/212°F, when the surface of the liquid will continuously show bubbles.

CARAMELISE To slowly heat sugar until it turns to liquid and goes brown.

CHOP To cut food into small pieces with a sharp knife.

COAT To cover food with a protective coating, such as batter, breadcrumbs or flour, before frying or covering food with a sauce.

CORE To remove the hard, indigestible centre of some foods, such as peppers, kidneys, apples, pears, pineapples.

CREAM To beat together fat and sugar until the mixture is pale and fluffy and resembles whipped cream.

CRUSH To break down food into smaller particles.

DICE To cut food into small, even-sized, cube-shaped pieces.

DISSOLVE To mix a dry or solid ingredient with a liquid, applying heat if necessary, until the mixture is clear.

DRAIN To remove any liquid or fat from foods by using a sieve, colander or draining spoon, or by placing food on absorbent kitchen paper.

DRY-FRY To fry without the use of extra fat or oil.

DUST To sprinkle food lightly with flour, sugar or other dry ingredient.

FLAKE To separate cooked fish into small pieces using two forks.

FLAMBÉ To ignite and burn a liqueur, which has been poured over food, to add the flavour of the alcohol.

FOLD To mix a whisked or whipped food with other ingredients, using a large metal spoon to cut through and then gently lift up, so that the mixture retains its lightness.

FRY To cook food in hot fat or oil, either by immersing it completely or cooking in a little fat and turning the food.

GLAZE To give a glossy surface to a sweet or savoury dish.

GRATE To shave food into small shreds using a grater.

HULL To remove the calyx and stem from soft fruit.

KNEAD To combine ingredients, by hand, which are too stiff to stir.

LINE To add a protective covering to the base and/or to the sides of a cooking tin or dish.

MASH To beat or crush a soft mixture free from lumps, using a potato masher or fork.

MIX To combine two or more ingredients together, using your hands, a spoon, fork, knife, electric mixer or food processor, depending on the ingredients.

PARE To thinly peel fruit or vegetables.

PEEL To remove the outer rind or shell from a food.

POACH To cook food in a liquid at a temperature of not more than 96°C/205°F so that the surface is just trembling.

ROLL OUT To flatten pastry or dough, using a rolling pin.

RUB IN To incorporate fat into flour until the mixture resembles fine breadcrumbs.

SAUTÉ To fry lightly in a little butter and/or oil.

SCRAPE To remove the outer layer of food.

SEAL To fry meat or poultry in hot fat to give colour and add flavour and to encase a filling in pastry or other casing.

SEGMENT To remove the skin of citrus fruits and divide the flesh into natural portions.

SEPARATE To divide or separate one thing from another, such as the white of an egg from the yolk.

SHRED To cut food finely using a sharp knife.

SIFT To shake a dry ingredient, such as flour, through a sieve to remove any lumps.

SIMMER To cook food in a liquid kept just below boiling point.

SKIN To remove the outer coat or skin of a food.

SLICE To cut food into thin rounds or slices, using a sharp knife or food processor.

STIR To mix food gently in a circular movement, usually with a spoon.

STIR-FRY To cook thinly sliced foods quickly in a little very hot oil, in a wok or large frying pan, and stirring constantly.

STRAIN To pass a liquid through a sieve, colander or muslin cloth to remove any solids.

SWEAT To cook cut up vegetables in a little fat over a gentle heat, covered, to dry out their juices.

TOSS To turn or flip food over lightly to coat with flour, seasoning or dressing.

TURN OUT To remove food from a tin in which it was cooked or a mould in which it was set. The turned-out food should retain its shape.

WHIP To beat a food or mixture, using a fork, balloon whisk, rotary whisk or electric whisk, until it is light and fluffy due to the incorporation of air.

WHISK To introduce air into egg whites, using a balloon whisk, rotary whisk or electric whisk, to increase their volume. Whisked egg whites should hold their shape.

ZEST To remove the coloured part of the rind of citrus fruits.

About the Recipes

Here are a few notes about the recipes:

Metric and imperial quantities are given in the recipes but never mix together as they are not interchangeable.

Sets of measuring spoons are available in both metric and imperial sizes to give accurate measurements of small quantities.

Spoon measures are level.

Medium eggs are used in the recipes unless otherwise specified.

Basic Cooking Equipment

Having the right tool for the job really does make cooking easier and more pleasurable. Use this list as a guide to suit your needs.

Pots and Pans

very large saucepan
2 or 3 large pans with lids
non-stick milk pan
large frying pan or wok
  with a lid
non-stick omelette and
  pancake pan

Baking Dishes and Tins

2 round or oval ovenproof
  casserole dishes
gratin dish
pie dish
baking tray
Swiss roll tin
bun tray
roasting tin
20 cm (8 in) flan ring
  or tin
2 sandwich tins
wire cooling rack

Cutlery and Tools

wooden spoons
20 cm (8 in) long sharp
  knife
12 cm (5 in) vegetable or
  paring knife
bread knife
vegetable peeler with a
  swivel blade
forks
knives
tablespoons
teaspoons
slotted spoon
fish slice
spatula
cooking tongs
ladle
potato masher
skewers
apple corer
corkscrew
balloon whisk or an
  electric whisk
kitchen scissors
pastry brush
melon baller
zester

General

chopping board
kitchen scales
measuring jug
measuring spoons
kettle
food processor
can opener
colander
rolling pin
kitchen scales
measuring jug
measuring spoons
mixing bowl
pudding basins
sieve
grater
set of pastry cutters

VEGET

DISHES

Pizza with Christmas Coleslaw *13*

**Cheese Soufflés with Stilton Sauce
and Tomato Bites** *14*

Zorba's Frittata *15*

Tricolour Pasta *16*

**Ricotta-stuffed Mushrooms
with Sweet Potatoes** *17*

Fruit and Vegetable Curry *18*

Pronto Penne with Red Pesto *19*

Pizza with Christmas Coleslaw

SERVES 2

Here's one for the kids to prepare – it's so easy and it will boost their confidence. You don't need to stick to the toppings in the recipe; try ham, mushrooms or whatever takes your fancy.

½ an onion
5 tablespoons olive oil
200g can chopped tomatoes
½ tablespoon tomato purée
½ tablespoon dried mixed herbs
2 red peppers
½ a green pepper
1 mozzarella cheese, weighing about 150g (5oz)
2 tomatoes
one 125g (4oz) pizza base
14 black olives
¼ a white cabbage
½ a red onion
1 red apple
juice of ½ a lemon
1 tablespoon cranberry sauce
50g (2oz) walnut pieces
salt and freshly ground black pepper

❶ Pre-heat the oven to 220°C/425°F/Gas 7.

❷ Very finely chop the onion. Heat a tablespoon oil in saucepan. Add the onion and fry until golden.

❸ Add the can of tomatoes, tomato purée, mixed herbs, salt and pepper. Bring to boil, and cook for 8–10 minutes.

❹ Slice the red and green peppers, discarding the core and seeds. Slice the mozzarella into semi-circles. Put the tomatoes in a bowl, cover with boiling water for about 30 seconds then plunge into iced water. Using a sharp knife, peel off the skins then slice the flesh.

❺ Put the tomato sauce on the pizza base. Arrange the red and green peppers around the outside of the pizza to give a scalloped effect. Inside that, arrange a circle of skinned and sliced tomatoes alternating with the mozzarella. Inside that arrange a circle of black olives. Drizzle over 1 tablespoon of olive oil and grind on black pepper.

6 Cook in the oven for 8–10 minutes until golden.

7 Meanwhile, slice the cabbage finely and put into a large bowl. Very finely slice the red onion. Cut the apple into quarters, core and slice. Mix together the remaining oil, lemon juice and cranberry sauce and pour over the cabbage. Roughly chop the walnuts and add with the apples and onion. Stir together and season with salt and pepper.

8 Take the pizza out of the oven and arrange on a plate. Put the coleslaw in a bowl and serve with the pizza.

Cheese Soufflés with Stilton Sauce and Tomato Bites

SERVES 2

Soufflés are not as difficult to make successfully as you might think and this recipe will give you perfect, creamy and delicious results every time.

25g (1oz) butter, plus extra for greasing
fine dry breadcrumbs, to dust
40g (1½oz) Gruyère cheese
25g (1oz) plain flour
½ teaspoon wholegrain mustard
a pinch of cayenne pepper
150ml (¼ pint) milk
2 eggs
2 tomatoes
1 tablespoon sweet sandwich pickle
1 tablespoon cream cheese
50ml (2fl oz) double cream
40g (1½oz) Stilton cheese
1 tablespoon chopped fresh parsley
salt and freshly ground black pepper
flat-leaved fresh parsley, to garnish

1 Pre-heat the oven to 230°C/450°F/ Gas 8. Butter 2 ramekin dishes and dust with fine breadcrumbs.

2 Grate the Gruyère cheese. Melt the butter in a pan, stir in the flour and cook for 30 seconds. Add the mustard and cayenne pepper. Gradually whisk in the milk and cook until thickened. Stir in the Gruyère cheese and remove the pan from the heat.

3 Separate the eggs, putting the whites into a large clean bowl. Stir the yolks into the cheese mixture and check the seasoning. Using an electric whisk, whisk the egg whites until stiff. Using a large metal spoon, fold into the cheese mixture then divide the mixture between the ramekin dishes. Run a finger around the rim of each ramekin to give the soufflés a 'top hat' appearance when cooked. Place on a baking tray and bake in the top of the oven for 10–11 minutes until risen and golden brown.

❹ Meanwhile, cut the tops off the tomatoes, scoop out the seeds and drain upside down on kitchen paper. Mix together the pickle and cream cheese and use to fill the tomatoes. Place the lids on top at a jaunty angle and garnish each with a parsley leaf.

❺ Gently heat the cream in a saucepan and crumble in the Stilton cheese. Stir until the cheese has melted and season with pepper. Stir in the chopped parsley.

❻ Take the soufflés out of the oven and place in the centre of serving plates. Arrange the tomatoes around the dishes. Just before eating, lift the lid off the soufflés and pour a little of the Stilton sauce into the middle.

Zorba's Frittata

SERVES 2

Here's a simple way of dressing up an omelette. This colourful dish contains lovely Mediterranean flavours that sit well together.

1 onion
3 tablespoons olive oil
25g (1oz) butter
100g (4oz) small new potatoes
1 medium courgette
50g (2oz) spinach leaves, stalks removed
4 eggs
1 tablespoon chopped fresh parsley, plus extra to garnish
1 tablespoon chopped fresh mint
50g (2oz) feta cheese
2 ripe tomatoes
1 small red onion
a handful of pitted black olives
juice of ½ a lemon
salt and freshly ground black pepper

❶ Pre-heat the grill.

❷ Finely slice the onion. Then heat 2 tablespoons of the olive oil and the butter in a frying pan, add the onion and fry until softened.

❸ In a food processor, thinly slice the potatoes and add to onion. Cook for a further 5 minutes or until just tender, stirring occasionally. Thinly slice the courgette in the food processor and finely chop the spinach. Add to the pan and cook for a further 2–3 minutes until well combined and the spinach has wilted.

❹ Meanwhile, put the eggs, parsley and mint in a bowl and crumble in the feta. Whisk until well combined and season to taste with salt and pepper. Pour the eggs into the pan and cook for 2 minutes, pushing the mixture into the centre to allow the raw egg to flow down the edge of the pan.

5 When the omelette is lightly set, cook under the hot grill for a further 2–3 minutes until golden. Garnish with chopped parsley.

6 Meanwhile, cut the tomatoes into wedges and thinly slice the red onion. Put in a bowl with the olives and dress with the remaining olive oil and the lemon juice.

7 To serve, cut the omelette into wedges and serve at once with the tomato and onion salad.

Tricolour Pasta

SERVES 2

I've used double cream here for extra richness. Good mozzarella cheese is made from buffalo milk. Use this if you can, as the ones made from cow's milk are much more bland and rubbery.

1 small onion
1 tablespoon olive oil
175g (6oz) penne
2 eggs
2 tablespoons double cream
4 tablespoons freshly grated Parmesan cheese
salt and freshly ground black pepper
FOR THE TRICOLOUR SALAD
1 large ripe avocado
2 tomatoes
1 mozzarella cheese
1 tablespoon lemon juice
3 tablespoons olive oil
¼ teaspoon cracked black peppercorns
basil leaves, to garnish

1 Finely chop the onion. Heat the oil in a frying pan, add the onion and fry until softened.

2 Put the pasta in a large saucepan of boiling salted water and cook for about 6 minutes or according to the instructions on the packet.

3 Meanwhile, prepare the salad. Cut the avocado in half then remove the stone and skin. Slice each avocado half. Slice the tomatoes and mozzarella cheese. Arrange the salad on 2 plates, alternating the colours. Drizzle over the lemon juice and oil. Sprinkle over the cracked peppercorns and garnish with basil leaves.

4 Beat the eggs in a bowl with the cream and 3 tablespoons of the Parmesan cheese. Season with salt and pepper to taste.

5 Drain the pasta and return to the pan. Tip in the onion and the egg mixture and return to the heat. Cook for about 30 seconds and then remove from the heat. Pile the pasta on to serving dishes and garnish with more basil and the remaining Parmesan cheese. Serve with the tricolour salad.

Ricotta-stuffed Mushrooms with Sweet Potatoes

SERVES 2

Sweet potato can be used for savoury or sweet dishes. The root vegetable originated from Peru, but is now grown in Africa and the West Indies as well. Try it, you'll be surprised by its delicious taste.

250g (8oz) sweet potato, peeled
4 tablespoons olive oil
2 large open flat mushrooms, about 10cm (4in) in diameter
40g (1½oz) freshly grated Parmesan cheese
175g (6oz) ricotta cheese
¼ teaspoon freshly grated nutmeg
1 egg yolk
1 tablespoon chopped fresh parsley
½ a small onion
275g (10oz) can chopped tomatoes
2 teaspoons of tomato purée
a good splash of dry white wine or water
50g (2oz) canned haricot beans or cannellini beans
2 teaspoons green pesto sauce
salt and freshly ground black pepper
a few sprigs of fresh rosemary, to garnish

Sweet Potatoes *Despite their name, sweet potatoes are not related to potatoes although they are a tuber vegetable and are prepared and cooked in the same way. They are an elongated shape with a white or purplish red skin and the flesh is orange or white. They taste sweet and are slightly perfumed.*

1 Pre-heat the oven to 220°C/425°F/Gas 7.

2 Cut the sweet potato into 1cm (½in) dice. Pour 2 tablespoons of olive oil into a roasting dish and add the sweet potatoes. Sprinkle with salt and pepper and turn in the oil. Roast on the top shelf of the oven for 15 minutes.

3 Meanwhile, carefully trim the stalks from the mushrooms and set aside. Mix ¾ of the Parmesan cheese into the ricotta. Season with nutmeg, salt and pepper. Add the yolk and chopped parsley.

4 Spoon the cheese mixture on to the mushrooms, leaving a clear edge of mushroom all around. Sprinkle over the remaining Parmesan cheese and bake in the oven for 10 minutes.

5 Meanwhile, heat 1 tablespoon of olive oil in a saucepan. Add the onion and cook for 1 minute. Chop the stalks of the mushrooms and add to the pan. Add the chopped tomatoes, tomato purée, wine and season with salt and pepper.

6 Take the sweet potato from the oven, turn and return to the oven.

7 Mix together the beans, pesto and remaining olive oil. Set aside.

8 Pour the tomato sauce into a food

processor or blender and process until smooth. Flood the serving plates with the sauce and dot the beans around the edge of the sauce. Serve the sweet potato dotted around the edge of the plates with the beans. Take the mushrooms from the oven, place one in the centre and garnish with a sprig of rosemary.

Fruit and Vegetable Curry

SERVES 2

How often do you see people order curry and then pile lots of fruit and nuts on top? This dish has it all in one pot and the fruit, vegetables and spices complement each other beautifully.

100g (4oz) basmati rice
2 tablespoons flaked almonds
1 onion
100g (4oz) cauliflower
100g (4oz) green beans
2 tomatoes
2 tablespoons vegetable oil
1 garlic clove
2 teaspoons ginger purée
1 tablespoon medium curry paste
300ml (½ pint) vegetable stock
1 tablespoon tomato purée
175g (6oz) cooked potato
1 banana
1 apple
1 tablespoon sultanas
a squeeze of lemon juice (optional)
a small handful of fresh coriander
150ml (¼ pint) natural yogurt
1 tablespoon desiccated coconut
salt and freshly ground black pepper
sprigs of fresh coriander, to garnish

❶ Rinse the rice well then add to a saucepan of boiling water and cook according to the instructions on the packet.

❷ Heat a dry frying pan over a moderately high heat. Add the flaked almonds and dry-fry for 1–2 minutes until golden. Take off the heat and set aside.

❸ Cut the onion in half then thinly slice. Cut the cauliflower into bite-sized florets. Trim the green beans and cut into 5cm (2in) lengths. Cut the tomatoes into wedges.

❹ Heat the oil in a saucepan. Add the onion and cook for 2 minutes. Crush the garlic and add to the onion with the ginger purée and curry paste. Cook for 1 minute. Add the vegetable stock, tomato purée,

Apples and Bananas *When using apples and bananas, prepare them just before use as, once they are exposed to the air, they turn brown. Brushing with lemon juice will help to prevent browning.*

cauliflower, green beans, tomatoes, salt and pepper and cook for 3 minutes.

5 Cut the potato into 2cm (¾in) chunks. Chop the banana. Core and dice the apple. Add half the apple and banana to the pan with the sultanas and cooked potato. Simmer for 3–5 minutes. Season with salt and pepper and a squeeze of lemon if you wish.

6 Chop the coriander. Drain the rice and stir in the coriander with the toasted almonds.

7 Mix the remaining banana and apple into the yogurt and stir in the coconut. Spoon into a serving bowl to serve with the curry. Pile the rice on to serving plates. Make a well in the centre and the curry on top. Garnish with sprigs of fresh coriander.

Pronto Penne with Red Pesto

SERVES 2

Sun-dried tomatoes have an intense flavour that can bring life to any dish. They are now widely available. The sun-dried tomato purée may not be as easy to get hold of – ask your local supermarket to stock it.

225g (8oz) penne
1 red pepper
about 120ml (4fl oz) olive oil
2 tablespoons pine kernels
1 large ripe plum tomato
50g (2oz) block of fresh Parmesan cheese
2 tablespoons sun-dried tomato purée
1 small fresh red chilli
3 sun-dried tomatoes in oil, drained
1 fresh basil plant, about 15g (½oz) of leaves
2 garlic cloves
1 ciabatta roll
salt and freshly ground black pepper

Penne *are small, hollow pasta shaped like quills with angled ends. They are available plain and ridged but if you're unable to find them, other tubular pasta can be used here.*

1 Pre-heat the grill and heat a small frying pan.

2 Put the penne in a saucepan of boiling salted water and cook for 8–10 minutes until just tender.

3 Meanwhile, cut the pepper into quarters, remove the seeds and core and brush the flesh with a little of the oil. Place on a grill rack and grill until the skin is blackened.

4 Put the pine kernels in the frying pan and cook over a moderate heat until toasted, stirring occasionally. Leave to cool a little.

5 Using a sharp knife, cut a cross on the bottom of the tomato and place on a long fork. Hold directly into the gas flame, protecting your hand with a tea-towel, until the skin has blackened slightly. Leave to cool a little, remove the skin and discard.

6 Remove the pepper from the grill pan and, using tongs, place in a polythene bag. Trap in some air and secure tightly. Set aside.

7 Grate 25g (1oz) of the cheese and put in a food processor with the tomato purée and pine kernels. Cut the chilli in half, remove the seeds and add the flesh to the food processor with the tomato and sun-dried tomatoes. Mix until finely chopped. Pick all the basil leaves off the plant, reserve a few to garnish and add to the food processor with 1 of the garlic cloves. Mix until finely chopped then season well with salt and pepper.

8 Heat a griddle or large frying pan.

9 Remove the pepper from the bag, peel off the skin and discard. Add to the food processor and chop finely. Blend until smooth, then slowly add (75ml/3fl oz) of the oil and about 1 small jug of water to make a sauce.

10 Slice the ciabatta roll, drizzle with the remaining oil and char the bread in the griddle on both sides until toasted. Cut the remaining garlic clove in half and use to rub all over the slices of bread.

11 Drain the cooked penne, return to the pan and toss with the red pesto. Pile the penne into a serving dish and garnish with the reserved basil leaves and some Parmesan shavings. Serve at once with the charred bread.

FISH
DISHES

**Thai Salmon Fillets with Coconut Rice
and Oriental Vegetables** 22

Goan Fish Curry with Spicy Vegetables 23

Spicy Fish Balti with Sweet Lassi 24

Salmon en Croûte 25

Pan-fried Pizza Marinara 26

Good Fish Pie 27

Smoked Salmon and Avocado Tagliatelle 28

Smoked Fish Cakes with Vegetable Ribbons 29

Salmon Rösti with Tartare Sauce 30

**Blackened Salmon Fillet on a Bed
of Hot and Sour Lentils** 31

Aubergine Stacks with Caesar Salad 32

Spiced Fish with Tabbouleh 33

Sweet and Sour Cod Nuggets 34

Thai Salmon Fillets with Coconut Rice and Oriental Vegetables

SERVES 2

Coconut is available in supermarkets and comes in different forms: in cans, packets or blocks. If you use fresh coconut, don't use the water inside. You'll need to grate the hard flesh, infuse with tap water and strain slowly.

---

3 tablespoons sunflower oil
1 teaspoons Thai red curry paste (available in jars)
grated rind and juice of 2 limes
two 175g (6oz) salmon fillets (cut into a square)
150ml (¼ pint) coconut milk
100g (4oz) Thai jasmine rice
100g (4oz) baby sweetcorn
1 carrot
½ a leek
2cm (¾in) piece of fresh root ginger
½ a fresh red chilli
100g (4oz) mange-tout peas
½ teaspoon dried lemon grass, plus 1 long piece of fresh
2 tablespoons light soy sauce
salt and freshly ground black pepper
1 lime and fresh coriander, to garnish

❶ Mix 2 tablespoons oil, the Thai curry paste, lime rind and juice, salt and pepper in a shallow dish. Add the salmon fillets and turn to coat in the marinade. Set aside to marinate.

❷ Put the coconut milk and 300ml (½ pint) water in a saucepan and bring to the boil. Add the rice, cover and simmer for 10–12 minutes until the rice is tender and all of the liquid has been absorbed.

❸ Cut the sweetcorn in half lengthways. Cut the carrot and leek into thin julienne strips, about 5cm (2in) in length. Grate the ginger. Halve the chilli, remove the core and seeds then finely chop the chilli flesh.

❹ Pre-heat a griddle pan or grill. Add the marinated salmon fillets and cook for 6–8 minutes, turning once, until cooked through.

❺ Heat the remaining tablespoon of oil in a wok. Add the baby sweetcorn, mange-tout, carrot, leek, ginger, chilli and lemon grass and stir-fry for 2 minutes. Add a little of the marinade juices. Add the soy sauce and stir-fry for a further 1 minute.

❻ Spoon the cooked rice into lightly oiled ramekin dishes, then carefully turn out on to serving plates. Spoon the stir-fried vegetables next to the rice and then place the salmon on top of the vegetables. Using a zester, cut shreds of lime rind and scatter over the salmon fillets, with a little fresh coriander, to garnish.

Goan Fish Curry with Spicy Vegetables

SERVES 2

To combine two starchy foods such as potatoes and rice in the same dish may seem a little strange but it works to perfection here. If you can't get haddock or fancy a change, try hoki, which is a white fish similar to cod in taste.

225g (8oz) potato, peeled
100g (4oz) basmati rice
2 cardamom pods (optional)
½ an onion
2–3 garlic cloves
1½ tablespoons vegetable oil
75g (3oz) aubergine
100ml (4fl oz) coconut milk
2 tablespoons tikka paste
1 bay leaf
1 small red pepper
1 teaspoon curry powder
½ teaspoon cumin seeds
a large handful baby spinach leaves
grated rind and juice of 1 lemon
1 tablespoon chopped fresh coriander leaves
225g (8oz) haddock fillet or hoki
1 teaspoon red wine vinegar
½ teaspoon sugar
salt and freshly ground black pepper

❶ Put 2 saucepans of salted water on to boil, cut the potato into 2cm (¾ in) chunks, add to 1 pan and simmer for 8 minutes. Rinse the rice and put into the second pan.

Crack the cardamom pods, add to the rice and cook according to the instructions on the packet.

❷ Chop the onion and the garlic. Heat the vegetable oil in a large frying pan, add the onion and half the garlic and fry gently. Cut the aubergine into cubes and add to the pan.

❸ Put the coconut milk into a saucepan, add the tikka paste, the remaining garlic and the bay leaf and heat through gently. Slice the pepper and add to the coconut milk. Add the curry powder and cumin and stir together.

❹ Drain the potatoes and add to the aubergine mixture then add the spinach, lemon rind, 1 tablespoon lemon juice, the coriander and season with salt and pepper.

❺ Cut the fish into 2cm (¾ in) cubes and add to the coconut milk.

❻ Drain the rice and return to the pan, off the heat, to keep warm.

❼ When the fish is tender, add the vinegar, 2 teaspoons lemon juice and sugar and season with salt and pepper.

❽ To serve, pile the rice on to serving plates, put the vegetables to one side and the fish curry on top of the rice.

Spicy Fish Balti with Sweet Lassi

SERVES 2

If you can't get cod, ask your fishmonger for a similar firm fish. Monkfish is ideal but on the expensive side. The secret is not to overcook the fish or it starts to break up. Lassi is the perfect accompaniment; if you want to make the drink savoury, add a teaspoon of salt instead of caster sugar.

225g (8oz) cod fillet, skinned
1 egg white
2 tablespoons seasoned flour
4 tablespoons sunflower oil
1 onion
1cm (½in) piece of fresh root ginger, peeled
1 garlic clove
2 tablespoons flaked almonds
1 small courgette
2 tablespoons balti curry paste
200ml (7fl oz) carton coconut cream
1 tablespoon caster sugar
4 mini garlic and coriander naan breads
175g (6oz) ice cubes
300ml (½ pint) natural yogurt
300ml (½ pint) milk
a pinch of ground cinnamon
a small bunch of fresh coriander
salt and freshly ground black pepper

Balti Pan *A balti pan is similar to a small wok but has two small handles. Use a wok if you do not have a balti pan or a large frying pan if you do not have a wok.*

❶ Pre-heat the oven to 200°C/400°F/ Gas 6. Heat a balti pan or wok.

❷ Cut the fish into 4cm (1½ in) pieces. Loosen the egg white with a little water then dip the fish in egg and dust with flour.

❸ Add the oil to the pan and swirl it around. Add the fish and cook for 1–2 minutes until opaque, stirring constantly to prevent sticking. Remove the fish with a slotted spoon and drain on kitchen paper.

❹ Chop the onion and finely chop the ginger and garlic. Add to the pan and stir-fry for 2–3 minutes. Meanwhile, heat a small frying pan and dry-fry the almonds until toasted.

❺ Cut the courgette in half lengthways then slice the flesh diagonally. Stir the curry paste into the pan and stir-fry for 30 seconds. Add the coconut cream, courgette and 1 teaspoon of the sugar and bring to the boil. Return the fish to the pan and cook for another 3–4 minutes.

❻ Meanwhile, place the naans on a baking tray and sprinkle with a little water. Place in the oven for 5 minutes until heated through.

❼ Meanwhile, make the lassi. Put the ice cubes in a blender or food processor with the yogurt, milk and remaining sugar. Blend until frothy and pour into tall glasses. Sprinkle with a little cinnamon.

8 Chop the coriander. Sprinkle the flaked almonds over the balti and scatter the coriander over the top. Place a napkin so that it's heaped up in the middle on a serving plate and then put the pan directly on top. Alternatively, spoon the spicy fish balti on to serving plates.

9 Remove the naans from the oven and break into pieces. Arrange around the balti pan or on the serving plates. Serve at once with the lassi.

Salmon en Croûte

SERVES 2

A simple dish that is a meal in one. Basmati rice is a slender long grain and is available in brown and white. Basmati means fragrant and, as its name implies, you get a distinctive aroma as well as good flavour.

2 lemons
15g (½oz) watercress
2 tablespoons mascarpone cheese
two 75g (3oz) salmon fillets (from the tail end)
2 sheets of frozen ready-rolled lattice puff pastry, thawed
1 egg, beaten
1 tablespoon sunflower oil
65g (2½oz) chilled unsalted butter
50g (2oz) button mushrooms
225g (8oz) cooked basmati rice
2 tablespoons toasted flaked almonds
2 tablespoons dry white wine
1 plum tomato
1 small bunch of fresh parsley
salt and freshly ground black pepper

1 Pre-heat the oven to 230°C/450°F/ Gas 8. Place a baking tray in the oven. Oil 2 ramekin dishes.

2 Grate the rind and squeeze out the juice from 1 lemon. Wash and finely chop the watercress. Put in a bowl with the mascarpone, a pinch of the lemon rind, salt and pepper and mix until combined.

3 Skin the salmon pieces and then divide the watercress mixture between the 2 pieces, spreading it evenly on top. Lay the pastry pieces, lattice side down, and place the salmon on top so that the watercress filling is enclosed between the pastry and salmon.

4 Brush all the edges with beaten egg and bring up the ends to meet over the salmon, trim off any excess with a pair of scissors. Fold over both of the sides to enclose the filling completely, using the trimmings if necessary. Press down to seal. Brush the parcels all over with beaten egg.

5 Remove the baking tray from the oven and place a piece of baking parchment on top. Using a fish slice, transfer the salmon parcels to the tray and bake for about 12 minutes until golden brown.

6 Heat the oil and 15g (½oz) butter in a frying pan. Slice the mushrooms, add to the pan and fry for 1–2 minutes until just beginning to soften. Add the rice and almonds and stir-fry until the rice is just heated through.

7 Put the wine and 1 tablespoon of lemon juice in a small pan and bring to a simmer. Dice the remaining butter and whisk in until well combined. Season with salt and pepper to taste.

8 Cut the tomato into quarters and remove the seeds. Cut thin slices, not quite up to the top of each quarter, and prise open into a fan.

9 Chop some of the parsley and add to the rice mixture with the remaining lemon rind. Season with salt and pepper to taste and stir until well combined.

10 Spoon the rice into the ramekin dishes and turn out on to serving plates. Garnish with the tomato fans. Add the salmon parcels and spoon around some of the sauce. Cut the remaining lemon into wedges and place 1 on each plate with a sprig of parsley. Serve at once.

Pan-fried Pizza Marinara
SERVES 2

Pizza is always a favourite with all the family and this home-made base is incredibly easy to make and cooks in a few minutes in the frying pan.

175g (6oz) self-raising flour
½ teaspoon dried mixed herbs
4 tablespoons olive oil
3 plum tomatoes
1 mozzarella cheese with basil in it, weighing about 150g (5oz)
3 tablespoons tomato pizza topping (from a jar)
75g (3oz) tuna fish chunks in brine
75g (3oz) peeled prawns
5 pitted black olives
a few anchovies (optional)
salt and freshly ground black pepper
a sprig of fresh basil, to garnish

1 Sift the flour and ½ teaspoon salt into a bowl. Add the dried herbs and a little pepper. Stir in 2 tablespoons of olive oil and then mix in 3 tablespoons of water to form a soft dough. Turn on to a floured board and knead until smooth.

2 Heat the remaining oil in a frying pan. Roll the dough into a round. Put the dough into the pan and fry over a moderate heat for 4 minutes. Turn the pizza over and cook on the other side for 4 minutes.

3 Meanwhile, put the plum tomatoes in a bowl, cover with boiling water for about 30 seconds then plunge into iced water.

Using a sharp knife, peel off the skins then slice the flesh. Slice the mozzarella cheese and set to one side.

4 Pre-heat the grill.

5 Spread the tomato pizza topping on top of the pizza dough and arrange the sliced tomatoes in an overlapping circle on top. Sprinkle on the tuna and prawns, dot with the olives and anchovies and finally arrange the slices of mozzarella on top.

6 Grill the pizza for 3–4 minutes until the cheese is bubbling and the tomatoes are cooked. Cut the pizza into slices and serve hot, garnished with a basil sprig.

Serving Suggestion *This pizza is particularly good served with coleslaw. Follow the recipe on page 13, omitting the cranberry sauce if preferred.*

Good Fish Pie

SERVES 2

Although I've recommended cod and haddock here, ask your fishmonger for some nice choice cuts for a fish pie. You'll be surprised by the good-quality cuts he might give you for a fraction of the normal price.

450g (1lb) potatoes, peeled
375ml (13fl oz) milk
1 bay leaf
a few black peppercorns
½ a small onion, sliced
2–3 parings of lemon rind
100g (4oz) cod fillet, skinned
100g (4oz) smoked cod or haddock fillet, skinned
2 hard-boiled eggs
25g (1oz) Cheddar cheese
25g (1oz) butter
15g (½oz) plain flour
1 tablespoon chopped fresh parsley
75g (3oz) peeled prawns
a pinch of freshly grated nutmeg
salt and freshly ground pepper
lemon slices, to garnish

1 Put the potatoes into a saucepan of cold salted water, bring to the boil and simmer until the potatoes are tender. To test, pierce the potatoes with a sharp knife.

2 Meanwhile, put 300ml (10fl oz) of the milk, the bay leaf, peppercorns, onion slices and lemon rind into a large frying pan and heat gently. When the milk is hot, add the fish and poach gently. Do not let the milk boil.

3 While the fish cooks, shell the eggs and slice into quarters. Grate the cheese.

4 When the fish just begins to flake when touched, lift out of the milk and put into a 20cm (8in) pie dish and flake into pieces.

5 To make the sauce, melt half the butter in a saucepan then stir in the flour and cook for 30 seconds. Strain the milk in which the fish was poached, on to the flour and butter and whisk continuously until the mixture thickens. Season with salt and pepper and add the chopped parsley.

6 Scatter the prawns over the fish, arrange the eggs over the prawns, then pour the sauce over the pie and gently stir.

7 Pre-heat the grill.

8 Drain the potatoes and mash with the remaining milk and butter. Add salt and pepper to taste and a pinch of the nutmeg.

9 Either pipe or spread the potato on to the pie, sprinkle with the cheese and place under a medium grill for 5–10 minutes until brown. Serve garnished with lemon slices.

Smoked Salmon and Avocado Tagliatelle

SERVES 2

The combination of smoked salmon and avocado is to die for, so my wife tells me when I make her this dish. You can get smoked salmon trimmings from your fishmonger without having to pay the earth.

175g (6oz) tagliatelle
2 shallots
4 tablespoons olive oil
15g (½oz) butter
1 garlic clove
3 tablespoons white wine
150ml (¼ pint) crème fraîche
1 ripe avocado
1 tablespoon chopped fresh dill
100g (4oz) mixed Italian lettuce leaves
25g (1oz) pitted black olives, halved
15g (½oz) sun-dried tomatoes in oil
1 tablespoon white wine vinegar
½ teaspoon Dijon mustard
a pinch of caster sugar
100g (4oz) smoked salmon trimmings
2 tablespoon grated Parmesan cheese
salt and freshly ground black pepper

1 Put the pasta in a saucepan of boiling water and cook for 8 minutes until just tender.

2 Meanwhile, finely chop the shallots. Heat 1 tablespoon of oil and the butter in a frying pan, add the shallots and cook for 3 minutes. Crush the garlic and add to the shallots. Stir in the wine and cook for 1 minute. Add the crème fraîche and simmer gently for 3 minutes.

3 Meanwhile, cut the avocado in half lengthways, remove the stone and peel off the skin. Place each avocado half, cut-side down, then cut widthways into slices.

4 Add the avocado slices, chopped dill, salt and pepper to the sauce and cook gently for 2 minutes.

5 Put the lettuce leaves and olives in a bowl. Cut the sun-dried tomatoes into thin strips and add to the lettuce. Whisk together the 3 remaining tablespoons of olive oil, the vinegar, mustard, sugar, salt and pepper. Pour over the salad and toss together.

6 Cut the smoked salmon into strips, add to the sauce and heat gently. Drain the pasta, add to the avocado and smoked salmon sauce and toss together gently.

7 Pile the tagliatelle on to serving plates, sprinkle over the Parmesan cheese and serve with the olive and sun-dried tomato salad.

Smoked Fish Cakes with Vegetable Ribbons

SERVES 2

Smoked fish has a lovely flavour and isn't all that expensive. If the breadcrumbs are too fresh, you can always dry them out in a low-heated oven for 5–10 minutes.

225g (8oz) smoked cod or haddock fillet, skinned
225g (8oz) mashed potatoes
a small handful of fresh parsley, chopped
1 egg yolk
grated rind of 1 small lemon
50g (2oz) seasoned flour
1 egg, beaten
50g (2oz) dried undyed breadcrumbs
olive oil, for frying
1 large carrot
1 large courgette
25g (1oz) butter
100ml (4fl oz) tomato pasta sauce
1 tablespoon capers
salt and freshly ground black pepper
lemon wedges, to garnish

1 Chop or flake the fish into a bowl. Add the mashed potatoes, parsley, egg yolk, lemon rind, salt and pepper. Mix well and form into 4 patties.

2 Dip each fish cake into flour, beaten egg then breadcrumbs. Heat a little oil in a frying pan, add the fish cakes and fry gently for 3 minutes on each side.

3 Using a vegetable peeler, shave long strips from the carrot and courgette. Melt the butter in a saucepan and briefly cook the vegetable ribbons. Do not over-cook or the ribbons will break up. Season with salt and pepper.

4 Heat the tomato pasta sauce in another saucepan and add the capers.

5 To serve, spoon some of the tomato sauce on to serving plates, place 2 fish cakes on top and serve the vegetable ribbons to the side. Garnish with lemon wedges.

Quantities *If you wish to make this recipe for 4 people, simply double the quantities.*

Salmon Rösti with Tartare Sauce

SERVES 2

If you like that lovely, salty, sharp flavour that capers offer, try adding a few chopped anchovies to the tartare sauce, for a truly magnificent experience.

two 225g (8oz) cooked waxy potatoes, peeled
2 spring onions
200g (7oz) can red salmon, drained
25g (1oz) unsalted butter
4 tablespoons mild olive oil
2 tablespoons mayonnaise
2 tablespoons crème fraîche
1 teaspoon capers, rinsed
1 cocktail gherkin
a selection of herbs, such as chives, parsley, tarragon and chervil
a good pinch of paprika
2 thick slices of white bread
1 garlic clove
50g (2oz) mixed green salad leaves
5 cherry tomatoes
1 tablespoon freshly grated Parmesan cheese
salt and freshly ground black pepper

❶ Coarsely grate the potatoes and put in a bowl. Finely chop the spring onions and add to the bowl. Season with salt and pepper. Roughly flake the salmon and add to the potato mixture. Mix well to combine.

❷ Put the potato mixture on the work surface and divide into 4 pieces. With wet hands, shape the mixture into patties.

❸ Heat a large frying pan then add half the butter and half the oil. Add the patties to the pan and press down with a fish slice. Cook for 6–8 minutes, turning occasionally, until crisp and golden.

❹ Meanwhile, in a small bowl, mix together the mayonnaise and crème fraîche. Finely chop the capers and gherkin and add to the bowl. Put some sprigs of each herb in a small cup and snip with scissors until finely chopped. Stir into the mayonnaise mixture and add the paprika and season to taste with salt and pepper.

❺ Remove the crusts from the bread and cut the bread into cubes. Slice the garlic. Heat the remaining butter and oil in a small frying pan, add the croûtons (bread) and garlic, stirring to coat. Fry for 3–4 minutes until golden, stirring occasionally.

❻ Tear the lettuce leaves into bite-sized pieces and arrange on serving plates. Cut the cherry tomatoes in half and scatter on top of the lettuce.

❼ Arrange 2 salmon rösti on each plate and add a dollop of the tartare sauce. Scatter the croûtons and Parmesan cheese over the salad and serve at once.

Blackened Salmon Fillet on a Bed of Hot and Sour Lentils

SERVES 2

Lentils have been trendy for a while now and, with supermarkets making them available not only dried but also canned, eating healthily has never been easier. Balsamic vinegar does cost more, but the flavour is worth it.

½ an onion
vegetable oil, for frying
½ a red pepper
1 large garlic clove
2cm (¾in) piece of fresh root ginger, peeled
½ teaspoon ground cumin
420g (15oz) can lentils, drained
a few drops of Tabasco sauce
1 tablespoon tomato purée
a good splash of dry white wine
1 tablespoon balsamic vinegar
1 teaspoon soft brown sugar
225g (8oz) salmon fillet, skin on but scaled
¼ teaspoon ground turmeric
1 small head of fennel
125g (4oz) mange-tout peas
a small bunch of fresh coriander leaves
salt and freshly ground black pepper

❶ Finely chop the onion. Heat 1 tablespoon of the oil in a saucepan, add the onion and fry until softened.

❷ Meanwhile, dice the red pepper and add to the pan. Crush the garlic, grate the ginger and add with half the cumin and cook for 30 seconds. Add the lentils, Tabasco, tomato purée, wine, vinegar and sugar and cook gently.

❸ Meanwhile, cut the salmon fillet into 2 neat pieces. Rub the remaining cumin, the ground turmeric and a little salt into the skin.

❹ Heat a little vegetable oil in a heavy-bottomed frying pan and when it's hot add the salmon, skin side down (the skin should become crisp). Turn and seal the other side for 1 minute and then remove to a plate to rest (it should still be a little pink in the middle).

❺ Finely slice the fennel and cut the mange-tout diagonally. Heat a wok or large frying pan and add a little oil and the vegetables. Stir-fry until tender then season with salt and pepper.

❻ Season the lentils with salt and pepper. Chop the coriander leaves, reserving a few to garnish, and stir into the lentils at the last minute.

❼ Serve the salmon fillets on a bed of hot lentils with the fennel and the mange-tout to the side. Garnish with coriander leaves.

Aubergine Stacks with Caesar Salad

SERVES 2

Aubergines are an incredibly thirsty vegetable: the more oil you put in the pan the more they soak up. By grilling them you get the real flavour instead of the oily sponge. In other words calories, take five!

1 small aubergine
1 courgette
1 tablespoon olive oil
1 beefsteak tomato
100g (4oz) mozzarella cheese
2 teaspoons green pesto sauce
65g (2½oz) Parmesan cheese
4 tablespoons fresh breadcrumbs
1 egg
salt and freshly ground black pepper
FOR THE CAESAR SALAD
1 slice of bread
5 tablespoons olive oil
1 garlic clove
½ cos lettuce
1 egg yolk
1 tablespoon lemon juice
4 anchovies, snipped
salt and freshly ground black pepper

Caesar Salad *This famous salad originates from America. If serving to young children, pregnant women or elderly people, omit the raw egg.*

1 Pre-heat the oven to 200°C/400°F/ Gas 6. Put a griddle pan or frying pan over a high heat.

2 Trim the ends off the aubergine, then cut lengthways into 1cm (½in) thick slices. Slice the courgette. Brush the aubergine and courgette slices with the olive oil and season with salt and pepper. Cook on the pre-heated griddle pan for 3–4 minutes, turning once.

3 Meanwhile, cut the tomato and mozzarella cheese into 1cm (½in) thick slices.

4 Remove the aubergine and courgette slices from the griddle pan. Place half the aubergine slices on a baking tray. Arrange half of the courgette slices on top, over-lapping slightly. Put the tomato slices on top of the courgettes, then a layer of mozzarella cheese. Spread the pesto sauce over the mozzarella cheese. Top with the rest of the courgette and aubergine slices.

5 Grate all but 15g (½oz) of the Parmesan cheese and mix half with the breadcrumbs, salt and pepper. Sprinkle over the aubergine stacks. Cook in the oven for 10 minutes until the tops are golden.

6 Meanwhile, make the Caesar salad. Trim the crusts off the bread and discard. Cut the bread into 1cm (½in) cubes. Heat 2 tablespoons of olive oil in a small frying pan. Slice the garlic clove in half and add to

Thai Salmon Fillet with Coconut Rice and Oriental Vegetables *(page 22)*

Smoked Fish Cakes with Vegetable Ribbons *(page 29)*

Zorba's Frittata
(page 15)

Pizza with
Christmas
Coleslaw
(page 13)

**Jambalaya
with Tropical
Fruit Skewers**
(page 37)

**Viceroy's
Creamy
Chicken Curry
*(page 50)***

Tornado Tacos
(page 47)

Golden Turkey
Cordon Vert
(page 43)

Lemon Chicken and Asparagus Pasta
(page 44)

Medallions of Pork in a Mushroom Sauce
(page 65)

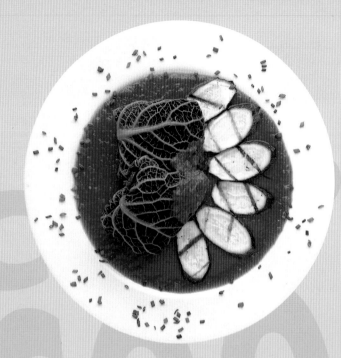

Cabbage
Parcels with
Tomato
Sauce
(page 59)

Beef
Stroganoff
(page 70)

Lamb and Pepper Kebabs with Creamy Haricot Beans *(page 61)*

Fusilli alla Carbonara with Herby Bread *(page 74)*

Fudgy Chocolate Pudding *(page 79)*

Mango and Coconut Fool with Brandy Snaps *(page 83)*

the oil. Add the cubes of bread and fry for 3 minutes, turning frequently, until golden.

7 Wash the lettuce leaves and tear into 2.5cm (1in) wide strips. Put in a bowl. Whisk together the egg yolk, lemon juice, remaining olive oil and black pepper. Pour over the lettuce leaves and toss together. Drain the croûtons on absorbent kitchen paper, sprinkle with salt then add to the lettuce with the anchovies and the rest of the grated Parmesan cheese.

8 Cook the egg in a saucepan of boiling water for 1 minute. Break the egg into the salad and toss well. Using a vegetable peeler, cut shavings of the remaining Parmesan cheese and scatter over the salad.

9 Put the aubergine stacks on serving plates and serve with the Caesar salad.

Spiced Fish with Tabbouleh

SERVES 2

People often get bulgar wheat, also known as burghul, and couscous mixed up. Bulgar wheat, when cooked, is a light, moist yet fluffy, nutty-tasting cracked wheat. Couscous is semolina grains coated with finer wheat flour.

100g (4oz) bulgar wheat
2 lemons
4–5 tablespoons olive oil
½ teaspoon mild chilli powder
1 teaspoon ground cumin
2 garlic cloves, crushed
½ teaspoon ground black and red pepper
2 tablespoons chopped fresh coriander
two 100g (4oz) haddock or cod fillet portions (from the tail end)
10cm (4in) piece of cucumber
2 plum tomatoes
1 bunch of fresh flat-leaved parsley
1 bunch of fresh mint
4 spring onions
plain flour, for dusting
salt and freshly ground black pepper

Bulgar Bulgar, also spelt bulghur, bulgur, burghul or burgul, is made from whole grains of wheat which are steamed, dried and then broken into pieces. It can be used in stuffings and salads, as it is here in the tabbouleh which is a traditional Lebanese salad.

1 Heat a frying pan on a low setting. Put the bulgar wheat in a bowl and pour over enough boiling water to cover completely. Set aside for 15 minutes or according to the instructions on the packet.

2 Meanwhile, squeeze the juice from 1 lemon. Put ½ the lemon juice and 2 tablespoons of the olive oil in a shallow non-metallic dish with the chilli powder, cumin, garlic, pepper and coriander.

3 Place the fish fillets in the dish, in a

33

single layer, and rub them all over with the spice mixture. Set aside to marinate.

❹ Meanwhile, quarter the cucumber and tomatoes, remove the seeds and dice both into a bowl. Add the remaining lemon juice and 2 tablespoons of the oil.

❺ Roughly chop the parsley and mint. Thinly slice the spring onions. Add the parsley, mint and spring onions to the bowl and toss together to coat in the dressing.

❻ Brush the frying pan with a little of the oil. Remove the fish from the marinade, shake off any excess oil and dust in some flour. Fry, skin-side down, for 2–3 minutes and then turn over and cook for another 1–2 minutes until just tender. Drain on kitchen paper and season with salt.

❼ Squeeze out any excess moisture from the bulgar wheat with your hands (it should still be moist) and add to the vegetable mixture. Stir to coat and season well with salt and pepper.

❽ Pile the tabbouleh into the middle of serving plates and place a piece of fish on top. Slice the remaining lemon and use to garnish. Serve at once.

Sweet and Sour Cod Nuggets

SERVES 2

Children generally like chicken or turkey nuggets, but once they've tried these cod nuggets with the tangy sauce the empty plates will speak for themselves.

8 tablespoons sunflower oil
225g (8oz) frozen cod nuggets
2 tablespoons white wine vinegar
2 tablespoons tomato ketchup
1 teaspoon soy sauce
150ml (¼ pint) chicken stock
1 small onion
50g (2oz) baby sweetcorn
50g (2oz) mange-tout peas
2 spring onions
50g (2oz) unsalted cashew nuts
275g (10oz) cooked long-grain rice
50g (2oz) frozen petits pois, thawed
1 egg, beaten
salt and freshly ground black pepper
spring onion curls, to garnish (see right)

❶ Heat a wok or large frying pan and a small saucepan. Add half the oil to the wok and heat until very hot. Shallow fry the cod nuggets for 5 minutes or until golden and tender.

❷ Meanwhile, put the vinegar in the pan and boil to reduce. Add the tomato ketchup, soy sauce and stock, bring to the boil and simmer for 2–3 minutes. Season with salt and pepper to taste.

❸ Slice the onion. Cut the sweetcorn and mange-tout in halves on the diagonal. Finely chop the spring onions.

❹ Using a slotted spoon, remove the cod nuggets from the wok and drain on kitchen paper. Drain off the excess oil, wipe out the wok and add 2 tablespoons of the oil. Add the onion and nuts to the wok and stir-fry for 1 minute. Then add the sweetcorn and cook for 2 minutes until just tender.

5 Heat the remaining oil in a frying pan. Add the rice, peas and salt and pepper. Stir-fry for 1 minute. Add the spring onions and cook for a further 1–2 minutes, tossing occasionally. Add the mange-tout to the wok and cook for 1–2 minutes.

6 Pour the egg, in a thin stream, into the rice mixture, stirring all the time. Cook for 1 minute until heated through.

7 Stir the sweet and sour sauce into the vegetables until coated. Toss in the cod nuggets and stir fry until just heated through.

8 Spoon the rice into Chinese bowls and arrange the cod mixture on top. Serve at once, garnished with the spring onion curls (see below).

Spring Onion Curls *To make, cut off the roots and discard most of the tops then cut each into 3 or 4 pieces. Using a sharp knife, cut down each piece of onion, taking care not to cut all the way down to the bottom so that the curl will hold together. Continue making as many cuts as possible. Put the curls into iced water for at least 20 minutes so that they open out. Drain before using as a garnish.*

POULTRY
DISHES

Jambalaya with Tropical Fruit Skewers *37*

Calabrian Chicken Bake *38*

Red Hot Drumsticks with Sweetcorn Skewers *39*

Chicken and Port Christmas Crackers *40*

New Year Chow Mein *41*

Jerk Chicken with Rice 'n' Peas *42*

Golden Turkey *Cordon Vert* *43*

Lemon Chicken and Asparagus Pasta *44*

Peking Duck *45*

Thai Chicken Curry *46*

Tornado Tacos *47*

Shredded Sesame Chicken *48*

Wholemeal Chicken and Ricotta Pancakes *49*

Viceroy's Creamy Chicken Curry *50*

Mexican Chicken with Guacamole *51*

Sauté of Chicken with Cider and Caramelised Apples *52*

Cannelloni Sorpresa *53*

Chinese Chicken with Egg-fried Rice *54*

Jambalaya with Tropical Fruit Skewers

SERVES 2

If you fancy the true taste of Southern American food, here it is in the form of Jambalaya. It's similar to gumbo or paella and is a one-pot sensation. Don't be put off by the many ingredients – the layers of flavour are superb.

1 onion
2 garlic cloves
1 celery stick
1 red chilli
½ red pepper
½ green pepper
2 tablespoons olive oil
1 chicken breast
1 chorizo sausage, weighing about 100g (4oz)
175g (6oz) quick-cook long-grain rice
½ teaspoon mild chilli powder
½ teaspoon turmeric
500ml (17fl oz) chicken stock (made from 1 cube)
100g (4oz) large cooked peeled prawns, thawed if frozen
salt and freshly ground black pepper
sprigs of fresh coriander, to garnish
FOR THE SKEWERS
25g (1oz) unsalted butter
1 tablespoon light muscovado sugar
2 limes
225g (8oz) mixed tropical fruit, such as pineapple, paw paw, mango, kiwi fruit, banana, papaya and Asian pears, cut into chunks and wedges

❶ Chop the onion and finely chop the garlic. Slice the celery. Finely chop the chilli, discarding the core and seeds. Slice the peppers into strips, discarding the core and seeds.

❷ Heat the oil in a large frying pan with a lid, add the onion and fry until it's beginning to soften. Add the celery, garlic and chilli and cook for a further 2 minutes.

❸ Meanwhile, cut the chicken into finger-length strips and slice the chorizo on the diagonal. Add to the pan with the pepper, stirring to coat.

❹ Add the rice, chilli powder and turmeric and cook for 2 minutes, stirring constantly. Pour in the stock and season to taste with salt and pepper. Bring to the boil, cover and simmer for 8–10 minutes or until the liquid is absorbed.

❺ Meanwhile, make the skewers. Melt the butter and sugar in a small saucepan, grate in the zest of 1 of the limes, then cut both in half and squeeze in the juice, reserving 1 half for decorating.

Tropical Fruit Salad *For convenience, you could buy a ready-prepared tropical fruit salad from a supermarket and use instead of the separate fruits.*

⑥ Heat a griddle pan. Arrange alternating pieces of different fruit on 15cm (6in) skewers and brush generously with the lime butter. Cook the skewers on the griddle pan for about 1 minute on each side, basting occasionally.

⑦ To serve, flood serving plates with the remaining lime butter and arrange the skewers on top. Slice the reserved lime and use to decorate the plates.

⑧ Add the prawns to the rice mixture and just heat through. Spoon the jambalaya on to the serving plates, garnish with the coriander and serve at once.

Calabrian Chicken Bake

SERVES 2

Pasta is energy food and chicken is easy to digest, so this dish makes an ideal supper! I always try to use fresh herbs, especially basil and parsley, as the dried varieties simply don't compare in taste.

200g (7oz) penne
2 skinless, boneless chicken breasts
2 tablespoons olive oil
1 medium onion, finely chopped
1 garlic clove, finely chopped
150g (5oz) mushrooms, sliced
a splash of white wine
225g (8oz) tub crème fraîche
1 tablespoon chopped fresh basil
1 tablespoon chopped fresh parsley
50g (2oz) Gruyère cheese, grated
1 avocado
3 plum tomatoes
1 tablespoon French dressing
salt and freshly ground black pepper

① Bring a large saucepan of salted water to the boil, add the pasta and cook according to the instructions on the packet. Drain well.

② Meanwhile, cut the chicken into bite-sized pieces.

③ Heat the oil in a frying pan, add the onion and garlic and fry for 1 minute. Add the chicken and fry for 3–4 minutes. Add the mushrooms and cook gently until the mushrooms are soft and the chicken thoroughly cooked.

④ Add the wine and cook for a further 1–2 minutes. Add the crème fraîche, basil and parsley and season with salt and pepper to taste.

⑤ Pre-heat the grill.

⑥ Mix the drained pasta and sauce together and put into an ovenproof dish. Sprinkle the grated cheese on top and place under the grill to brown.

⑦ To make the salad, halve the avocado, remove the stone and skin. Slice, leaving the thin end uncut and intact. Gently push the avocado into a fan. Slice the tomatoes and pour over some dressing. Serve the avocado and tomato with the pasta.

Red Hot Drumsticks with Sweetcorn Skewers

SERVES 2

Chicken drumsticks are such good value for money and can take on a variety of flavours. If corn is out of season or you're short of time, use frozen. You don't need to blanch them before grilling – just let them thaw out.

1 garlic clove
4 tablespoons tomato ketchup
1 teaspoon chilli sauce
1 teaspoon Worcestershire sauce
2 teaspoons clear honey
1 tablespoon chopped fresh tarragon
6 small chicken drumsticks, skinned
1 bay leaf
1 bouquet garni
1 corn on the cob
1 small red onion
8 cooked baby new potatoes
4 cherry tomatoes
2 tablespoons fresh lime juice
3 tablespoons olive oil
50g (2oz) mixed salad leaves

1 Crush the garlic and, in a small bowl, mix with the ketchup, chilli sauce, Worcestershire sauce, 1 teaspoon of the honey and half the tarragon.

2 Take 1 of the drumsticks and slip a knife in between the tendons and bone. Pull the knife up to expose the tendons and pull out (you may need tweezers to get rid of any stray ones). Pull off the skin and slash the flesh twice on each side. Repeat with the remaining drumsticks.

3 Put the drumsticks in a saucepan of boiling water with the bay leaf and the bouquet garni and poach for 3–4 minutes, then drain.

4 Pre-heat the grill. Line a grill rack with foil and arrange the drumsticks on it. Drizzle over half the sauce and grill for 5–6 minutes on each side until cooked through and charred.

5 Cut the corn on the cob into 8 slices, blanch in boiling water for 3 minutes then plunge into iced water. Slice the onion into 4 wedges.

6 Brush a griddle pan or frying pan with oil and heat. Thread the corn slices, onion wedges, new potatoes and cherry tomatoes on to four 15cm (6in) metal skewers.

7 Mix together the remaining honey and tarragon with 1 tablespoon each of the lime juice and oil and paint all over the skewers. Brush the pan with a little more of the oil and cook the skewers for 5–6 minutes, turning and basting frequently.

8 Tear the salad leaves into pieces and arrange on serving plates. Drizzle over the remaining lime juice and oil. Add the drumsticks, some of the sauce and 2 of the skewers to each plate. Serve at once.

Chicken and Port Christmas Crackers

SERVES 2

You don't have to wait until Christmas to try this dish. However, turkey is a good alternative to chicken. If you haven't used filo pastry before, this simple recipe shows you how.

2 cooked chicken breasts, finely chopped
2 spring onions, finely sliced
2 tablespoons port
1 tablespoon cranberry sauce
2 small sprigs of fresh rosemary
50g (2oz) butter
6 sheets of filo pastry
2 tablespoons sesame seeds
20 baby Brussels sprouts
8 cooked chestnuts
50g (2oz) Stilton cheese
175ml (6fl oz) double cream
lemon juice, to taste
salt and freshly ground black pepper

Filo Pastry *When using filo pastry, the secret is to keep the sheets covered with a clean damp tea-towel at all times as they crack if they become too dry.*

1 Pre-heat the oven to 200°C/400°F/Gas 6.

2 Mix together the chicken, spring onions, port, cranberry sauce and a few of the rosemary leaves, finely chopped. Season with salt and pepper.

3 Put the butter in a saucepan and heat gently until melted. Place one piece of filo pastry on top of another and brush with the melted butter. Put half the chicken mixture at one end and roll up. Repeat to make a second roll.

4 Cut the remaining 2 sheets of filo pastry in half. Close your fist and lay 1 sheet of pastry on top. Push the pastry partly into your fist, as a conjuror pushes a hanky into his fist, to form a fan. Repeat with the remaining pastry sheets. Tuck the pastry into both ends of the filo rolls to make 2 crackers.

5 Brush the crackers with melted butter and scatter sesame seeds over the top. Place on a baking tray and bake in the oven for 8–10 minutes until golden.

6 Meanwhile, cut a cross in the base of the sprouts then cook in boiling water for 5 minutes. Drain well. Put the chestnuts in boiling water to heat through then drain and toss in a little melted butter.

7 Crumble the Stilton cheese into a pan. Add the cream and heat, stirring, to make a sauce. Season with pepper and lemon juice.

8 Take the crackers out of the oven. Arrange on serving plates with the chestnuts and sprouts. Garnish with a sprig of rosemary. Serve the sauce on the side of the plates.

New Year Chow Mein

SERVES 2

I've always liked garnishes. Good presentation feeds the eye, which is half the joy of eating. You can buy ready-to-eat prawn crackers or dried prawn crackers which just need deep-frying.

4 baby carrots
50g (2oz) baby sweetcorn
½ a leek, washed and trimmed
2 tablespoons sunflower oil, for frying
225g (8oz) turkey pieces, prepared and packed for stir-frying
½ red pepper, sliced
25g (1oz) cashew nuts
1 garlic clove, finely chopped
1cm (½in) piece of fresh root ginger, finely chopped
50g (2oz) mange-tout peas
1½ sheets thread egg noodles
2 tablespoons soy sauce
100g (4oz) bean sprouts
2–3 tablespoons hoisin sauce
salt
1 spring onion and 2 radishes to garnish
prawn crackers, to serve

❶ Slice the carrots into strips or in half if they are very small. Slice the sweetcorn diagonally into 2cm (¾in) long pieces. Slice the leek into 4cm (1½in) strips.

❷ Bring a saucepan of water to the boil for the noodles. Heat a wok or a large frying pan.

❸ To prepare the garnish of spring onion, cut the spring onion into 3 or 4 pieces then, using a sharp knife, feather one end by making fine cuts at one end of each piece. Place in a bowl of iced water. Make 5 cuts around the radishes, almost to the stalk end, to form 5 petals.

❹ Put the oil in the wok. When hot, add the turkey and cook for 1 minute. When the turkey begins to loosen itself from the wok, stir in the carrots, pepper, cashew nuts, garlic and ginger.

❺ Add a little of the boiling water from the noodle pan to the stir-fry and steam-fry the vegetables for 1 minute. Add the leek and mange-tout.

❻ Add the noodles to the pan of boiling water and sprinkle with salt. Separate the noodles using chopsticks and cook according to packet instructions.

❼ Add the soy sauce to the stir-fry. Add the bean sprouts and hoisin sauce to the wok and stir.

❽ Drain the noodles and add to the wok. Stir together until all the noodles are well covered in the sauce.

❾ Serve in Chinese bowls garnished with the spring onion brushes and radish flowers. Accompany with prawn crackers and eat with chopsticks.

Jerk Chicken with Rice 'n' Peas

SERVES 2

Now here's one I made earlier. This is one recipe that is close to my heart because it's a real traditional Jamaican dish. Once you've tried jerk chicken, you'll keep going back for more.

1 bunch of spring onions
2 red chillies, preferably Scotch bonnet
3 tablespoons sunflower oil
½ teaspoon ground allspice
2 teaspoons light muscovado sugar
1 tablespoon cider vinegar
1 teaspoon ground paprika, plus extra for dusting
1 teaspoon fresh thyme leaves plus 4 thyme sprigs
2 chicken breast fillets, skinned
1 bay leaf
1 garlic clove
100g (4oz) easy-cook long-grain rice
300ml (½ pint) hot chicken stock
50g (2oz) sachet creamed coconut
400g (14oz) can red kidney beans
¼ of a red cabbage
¼ of a white cabbage
1 carrot
2–4 tablespoons mayonnaise
salt and freshly ground black pepper

❶ Finely chop the spring onions. Halve 1 of the chillies and remove the seeds.

❷ Put 3 of the spring onions and the chilli halves in a food processor with 1 tablespoon of the oil, the allspice, sugar, vinegar, paprika, thyme leaves and plenty of salt and pepper. Whizz until combined.

❸ Slash the chicken diagonally 4 times and place in a non-metallic dish with the chilli mixture. Stir to combine then set aside.

❹ Heat a frying pan. Heat 1 tablespoon of the oil in the pan. Add 2 of the spring onions, the remaining whole chilli, 1 thyme sprig and the bay leaf and crush in the garlic.

❺ Stir in the rice and cook for 1 minute, then pour in the stock and bring to a simmer. Finely chop the coconut and add to the pan with the kidney beans and their juice. Cover with a tight-fitting lid and simmer for about 10 minutes or until tender.

❻ Heat the remaining oil in a frying pan. Wipe off any excess marinade from the chicken pieces and add to the pan. Cook over a moderate heat for 8 minutes until lightly charred and tender, turning occasionally.

❼ To make the coleslaw, shred the cabbages and put in a bowl. Grate in the carrot and add the remaining spring onions. Season well with salt and pepper and stir in enough mayonnaise to coat.

❽ Arrange the chicken on serving plates. Spoon on some of the rice, discarding the chilli and thyme, and add a small spoonful of coleslaw. Garnish with a dusting of paprika and the thyme sprigs and serve at once.

Golden Turkey *Cordon Vert*

SERVES 2

Cooking with turkey couldn't be simpler. It has a subtle flavour which combines well with all kinds of herbs, spices and sauces to create such satisfying dishes as ... cordon vert.

350g (12oz) potatoes
2 tablespoons sunflower oil
½ a small leek, finely sliced
½ a celery stick, finely diced
a good pinch of dried thyme
25g (1oz) smoked ham, diced
½ tablespoon English mustard
75g (3oz) fresh breadcrumbs
2 turkey breast fillets
1 tablespoon sesame seeds
2 tablespoons seasoned flour
1 egg, beaten
25g (1oz) butter, plus a small knob
3 tablespoons milk
pinch of grated nutmeg
25g (1oz) red Leicester cheese, grated
100g (4oz) mange-tout peas
salt and freshly ground black pepper
lemon slices, to garnish

1 Cut the potatoes into 2cm (¾ in) chunks. Cook in a saucepan of boiling water for 10 minutes until tender.

2 Heat 1 tablespoon of oil in a pan, add the leek and cook for a further 2 minutes. Add the celery and thyme and cook for a further 2 minutes.

3 Spoon the leek and celery into a bowl. Add the ham, mustard, 4 tablespoons of the breadcrumbs, salt and pepper and mix well.

4 Cut the turkey fillets into two pieces. Put each piece of turkey between 2 pieces of clingfilm and flatten with a rolling pin to a thickness of about 5mm (¼ in). Spoon the leek and ham stuffing in the middle of each piece of turkey. Fold the turkey in half and seal the edges with cocktail sticks.

5 Mix the rest of the breadcrumbs and the sesame seeds together. Coat the turkey parcels in seasoned flour then dip in the beaten egg. Finally coat with the breadcrumbs and sesame seeds.

6 Heat the remaining 1 tablespoon oil and 15g (½oz) butter in a frying pan. Add the turkey parcels and cook for 6–8 minutes, turning once, until cooked through.

7 Meanwhile, drain the potatoes and mash with the remaining butter, the milk, nutmeg, salt and pepper. Stir in the grated cheese.

8 Boil the mange-tout peas in slightly salted water for 2 minutes. Drain well and toss in a knob of butter.

9 Put the turkey parcels on to plates and serve with the cheesy mashed potato and mange-tout peas. Garnish with a slice of lemon.

Lemon Chicken and Asparagus Pasta

SERVES 2

Asparagus range from the thin spear to the fattest jumbo. The buds should be tight, the spears an even colour, firm and unwrinkled. Avoid ones with woody stems which leave you with a lot of wastage. Asparagus is best cooked with the feet (the stalk end) in water and the heads in steam.

2 boneless, skinless chicken breasts
1 lemon
3 tablespoons olive oil
2 garlic cloves
175g (6oz) pappardelle (strips of pasta)
175g (6oz) asparagus
1 small leek, trimmed
1 small French stick, about 15cm (6in) long
a knob of unsalted butter
50g (2oz) baby plum tomatoes, sliced
1 tablespoon shredded fresh basil
150ml (¼ pint) double cream
1 teaspoon Dijon mustard
1 tablespoon freshly grated Parmesan cheese
salt and freshly ground black pepper

❶ Pre-heat the grill.

❷ Place the chicken in a non-metallic dish and grate over the zest of the lemon. Add 1 tablespoon of the oil, 1 crushed garlic clove, salt and pepper and toss to coat. Set aside.

❸ Put the pappardelle in a large saucepan of boiling salted water and cook for about 10–12 minutes until only just tender.

❹ Meanwhile, cut the asparagus into 4cm (1½in) lengths and cook in a pan of boiling salted water for 3–4 minutes or until just tender. Cut the leek into 5cm (2in) lengths then cut into thin shreds.

❺ Pre-heat the grill. Slice the bread and place on a grill rack. Toast on both sides.

❻ Heat a frying pan until very hot and then add 1 tablespoon of the oil and the butter. Quickly fry the chicken until lightly browned then squeeze over the juice of the lemon.

❼ Cut the remaining garlic clove in half and rub over the toast. Drizzle over the remaining oil and pile the tomatoes and basil on top. Season with salt and pepper to taste.

❽ Add the cream, mustard, shredded leek and Parmesan cheese to the pan. Cook until slightly thickened, stirring all the time. Add the asparagus to the chicken mixture. Drain the pasta thoroughly and add to the pan, tossing to coat.

❾ Spoon the chicken and pasta on to serving plates, garnish with the tomato toasts and serve at once.

Peking Duck

SERVES 2

This dish normally takes hours to prepare, but you can always trust me to find a short-cut. Ask your local supermarket to order the Chinese pancakes if you can't find them on the shelves. Remember, the stores want your business.

4 spring onions
1 teaspoon sesame oil
½ teaspoon ground ginger
½ teaspoon chilli purée
1 tablespoon white wine vinegar
1 tablespoon soy sauce
50g (2oz) plum sauce or jam
2 tablespoons clear honey
½ teaspoon Chinese five spice powder
two 175g (6oz) duckling breasts
5cm (2in) piece of cucumber
10 Chinese-style pancakes
cayenne pepper for dusting

❶ To prepare the garnish of spring onions, cut 2 of the spring onions into 3 or 4 pieces then, using a sharp knife, make fine cuts at one end of each piece. Put in a bowl of iced water to open out. Set aside.

❷ Heat the sesame oil in a small saucepan. Add the ginger and chilli and cook for 10 seconds, stirring. Add the vinegar, half the soy sauce and the plum conserve and heat gently until smooth and thickened, stirring occasionally.

❸ Mix together the honey, the remaining soy sauce and the Chinese five spice powder. Cut the duckling breasts in half lengthways and then cut into strips. Prick all over with a sharp knife and then coat all over with the honey mixture. Leave to marinate.

❹ Heat a wok or large frying pan.

❺ Meanwhile, cut the remaining 2 spring onions into 5cm (2in) pieces and shred them lengthways into thin strips. Cut the cucumber into 5cm (2in) pieces then cut the pieces into matchsticks, discarding the seeds.

❻ Add the duckling to the wok and stir-fry for 6–8 minutes until cooked through and tender, adding a little water if necessary.

❼ Remove the sauce from the heat and spoon into a small bowl.

❽ Place the pancakes in a steamer, standing over a pan of boiling water, and boil until just heated through.

❾ To serve, place a pancake on a plate and spread with a little of the plum sauce. Scatter the spring onion shreds and cucumber matchsticks down the middle and place the duckling slices on top. Roll up. Repeat with the remaining ingredients and arrange the pancakes on a serving plate. Garnish with the spring onion brushes and add a dusting of cayenne pepper.

Thai Chicken Curry

SERVES 2

The ready-made oriental mixes and pastes now available mean the tasty flavours of the East can be sampled in the comfort of your home.

100g (4oz) Thai jasmine rice or basmati rice
1 chicken stock cube
1 stalk of fresh lemon grass or 1 teaspoon dried
350g (12oz) boneless, skinnless chicken breasts
1 tablespoon sunflower oil
1 onion, chopped
1 fresh green chilli
2.5cm (1in) piece of fresh root ginger, grated
1 garlic clove, finely chopped
25g (1oz) creamed coconut
1 tablespoon green Thai curry paste
200ml (7fl oz) can coconut milk
juice of ½ a lime
1 teaspoon dark soy sauce
small handful of fresh coriander, chopped
salt and freshly ground black pepper
paprika, coriander sprigs, sliced cucumber and radish flowers (see right), to garnish

① Put the rice and crumbled stock cube in a saucepan of water. Bruise the lemon grass stalk and add to the pan. Bring the water to the boil and cook for about 10 minutes until the rice is tender.

② Cut the chicken breasts into 2cm (¾in) cubes. Heat the oil in a saucepan, add the chicken cubes and cook until golden. Add the chopped onion and cook for a further 2 minutes.

③ Meanwhile, finely chop the green chilli, discarding the core and seeds.

④ Add the ginger, garlic and chilli to the chicken and onion. Chop the creamed coconut. Add to the chicken with the Thai curry paste, coconut milk, lime juice, soy sauce, salt and pepper. Simmer for 5 minutes.

⑤ Drain the rice and remove and discard the lemon grass stalk. Spoon the rice on to serving plates. Stir the chopped coriander into the chicken just before serving and spoon on top of the rice. Sprinkle a little paprika over the rice. Garnish the curry with sprigs of coriander, cucumber slices and radish flowers.

Radish Flowers *To make a radish flower, make 5 cuts around the radish, almost to the stalk end, to form 5 petals all attached at the base. Put into a bowl of iced water and leave to open out.*

Tornado Tacos

SERVES 4

This Mexican recipe came about because I wanted to use up a few odd ingredients left in the fridge. My children and their friends still ask for it at tea time with looks of mouthwatering anticipation.

2 tablespoons sunflower oil
1 small onion, finely chopped
225g (8oz) minced turkey
1 small green pepper
1 teaspoon ground cumin
a good pinch of chilli powder
200g (7oz) can chopped tomatoes
200g (7oz) can red kidney beans, drained and rinsed
2 tablespoons tomato purée
150ml (¼ pint) vegetable stock (see below)
2 iceberg lettuce leaves
8 taco shells
1 small ripe avocado
1 small plum tomato
1 spring onion, finely chopped
a squeeze of lemon juice
a good pinch of garlic salt
4–6 tablespoons soured cream
salt and freshly ground black pepper
50g (2oz) Cheddar cheese, grated

Stock *For speed and convenience use a stock cube but, as they are usually very salty, use only half and add extra salt, if necessary, sparingly.*

1 Pre-heat the oven to 180°C/350°F/Gas 4.

2 Heat the oil in a frying pan, add the onion and fry for 2–3 minutes until softened. Add the mince and cook, stirring, for 2–3 minutes until browned.

3 Cut the green pepper in half and remove the core and seeds. Chop the flesh into small pieces and add to the pan with the cumin and chilli powder, stirring until combined. Add the tomatoes, kidney beans, tomato purée, stock, salt and pepper. Cook for 5 minutes or until thickened.

4 Roll up the lettuce leaves into a cigar shape, shred into thin ribbons and set aside.

5 Place the taco shells on a baking tray and bake for 2–3 minutes.

6 To make the guacamole, halve the avocado and remove the stone. Scoop out the flesh into a bowl and mash with a fork. Halve, seed and dice the tomato and stir into the avocado with the spring onion, squeeze of lemon, garlic salt, salt and pepper.

7 Remove the taco shells from the oven. Place some lettuce in the bottom of each one then spoon in a little of the mince mixture. Add a dollop of soured cream and the guacamole and sprinkle the cheese on top. Arrange on a serving plate and serve.

Shredded Sesame Chicken

SERVES 2

Unblended sesame oil has a rich light brown colour, keeps well and contains a substance that prevents it from going rancid. The toasted sesame oil that has a deep golden colour is used more as a seasoning or for marinades than cooking.

100g (4oz) basmati rice, rinsed well
1 teaspoon salt
1 tablespoon sesame oil
groundnut oil, for frying
1 egg white
2 teaspoons cornflour
100g (4oz) boneless, skinless chicken breast
75g (3oz) baby sweetcorn
100g (4oz) small broccoli florets
2 spring onions, sliced diagonally
2 teaspoons dark soy sauce
2 teaspoons cider vinegar
2 teaspoons sugar
2 tablespoons stir-fry yellow bean sauce
2 tablespoons dry sherry
½ teaspoon ground black and red pepper
2 tablespoons toasted sesame seeds

Basmati Rice *is the ideal rice to serve with Chinese and Indian dishes as it has a delicate, nutty flavour. It must be rinsed well before cooking to remove excess starch and prevent the grains from sticking together.*

1 Put the rice in a saucepan and add 300ml (½ pint) boiling water, ½ teaspoon of the salt and 1 teaspoon of the sesame oil. Cover and bring to the boil, then reduce the heat and simmer for 10–12 minutes.

2 Heat 2.5cm (1in) of groundnut oil in a wok or large frying pan.

3 Using a small whisk, mix together the egg white, cornflour and remaining salt until well combined. Using scissors, cut the chicken lengthways into thin strips then cut in half again. Stir into the egg white mixture.

4 Using tongs, add the coated chicken pieces, 1 at a time, to the wok and cook for 2–3 minutes until browned, stirring. Remove from the wok and drain on kitchen paper. Set aside.

5 Cut each sweetcorn diagonally into 3 pieces. Tip away all but 2 tablespoons of the oil from the wok and add the sweetcorn and broccoli. Sprinkle over about 2 tablespoons of water and stir-fry for 2–3 minutes until tender. Test by piercing with the tip of a knife.

6 In a bowl, mix together the spring onions, soy sauce, vinegar, sugar, yellow bean sauce, sherry, pepper and remaining sesame oil.

7 When the vegetables are tender, stir in half the sesame seeds and stir-fry for 30 seconds. Pour in the sauce and cook for 2 minutes. Return the chicken to the wok and toss until coated and heated through.

8 Fluff up the rice with a fork and spoon on to serving plates, making a well in the centre.

Add the sesame chicken, sprinkle over the remaining sesame seeds and serve at once.

Wholemeal Chicken and Ricotta Pancakes

SERVES 2

These pancakes are deliciously thick and satisfying: don't aim for paper-like crêpes!

50g (2oz) plain wholemeal flour
50g (2oz) plain white flour
2 teaspoons poppy seeds (optional)
1 egg, beaten
175ml (6fl oz) milk
1 small onion
75g (3oz) chestnut mushrooms
2 tablespoons olive oil, plus extra for frying
225g (8oz) stir-fry chicken strips
a good splash of dry white wine
100g (4oz) ricotta cheese
2 teaspoons wholegrain mustard
small handful of baby spinach leaves
salt and freshly ground black pepper

1 To make the pancake batter, put the flours and a pinch of salt into a bowl. Make a well in the centre and add the poppy seeds, if using, and the egg. Gradually add the milk and whisk into a smooth batter. Add 1 tablespoon water.

2 Chop the onion; slice the mushrooms. Heat a frying pan, add the 2 tablespoons oil and the onion and mushrooms and fry for

1 minute then add the chicken strips. Add the wine and simmer until the chicken is cooked.

3 Meanwhile, heat a non-stick frying pan. Add a little oil and when hot, pour in a quarter of the batter. Tip the pan so that the batter runs over the bottom of the pan. Cook over a high heat until the bottom is golden brown then turn the pancake over and cook the other side until golden. Cook 4 pancakes and keep warm by wrapping them in foil.

4 Stir the ricotta and mustard into the chicken mixture then add the spinach leaves. Stir until they have wilted. Season with salt and pepper.

5 To serve, spoon some of the chicken mixture on to each pancake, roll up and lift on to serving plates. Spoon any extra mixture over the top.

Serving Suggestion *These pancakes are particularly good served with a Caesar salad. See the recipe for Aubergine Stacks with Caesar Salad on page 32.*

Viceroy's Creamy Chicken Curry

SERVES 2

For those of you who like a rich, creamy coconut curry,
this one is definitely for you. Enjoy.

100g (4oz) basmati rice, well rinsed
½ teaspoon ground turmeric
2 tablespoons sunflower oil
1 large onion, weighing about 225g (8oz)
1–2 teaspoons garlic purée
225g (8oz) skinless, boneless chicken, cut into cubes
1 tablespoon mild curry paste
120ml (4fl oz) chicken stock
400g (14oz) can coconut milk
½ a cucumber
1 plum tomato
2 spring onions
150g (5oz) carton yogurt
1 tablespoon mango chutney
½ a small lemon
1 packet of mini poppadom crisps
a good pinch of paprika
salt and freshly ground black pepper

❶ Put the rice in a saucepan with the turmeric and 300ml (½ pint) boiling salted water and return to the boil. Cover and simmer for about 10 minutes.

❷ Heat the sunflower oil in a large frying pan. Thinly slice the large onion and add with the garlic purée. Fry over a medium heat until the onions are softened. Add the chicken to the pan and cook until just sealed.

❸ Add the curry paste and stir-fry for another minute. Pour in the stock, bring to the boil and boil fast until almost all the liquid has evaporated.

❹ Pour in two-thirds of the coconut milk and season generously with salt and pepper. Stir and simmer for about 6–8 minutes or until the chicken is cooked through and the sauce has thickened, adding more coconut milk if it's necessary.

❺ Cut the cucumber into quarters, remove the seeds, then finely chop. Finely chop the tomato and spring onions. Stir the cucumber, tomato and spring onions into the yogurt and season to taste with salt and pepper.

❻ Add the chutney to the chicken and squeeze in the lemon juice. Cook for a further 1–2 minutes.

❼ Pile the rice on to serving plates and spoon on some of the chicken mixture. Serve at once with the mini poppadoms and cucumber raita, sprinkled with a little paprika.

Mexican Chicken with Guacamole

SERVES 2

Occasionally a recipe comes along that touches the soul when indulged. Here's one of them. It goes down even better with a few Mexican beers or, dare I say, a Margarita or two?

225g (8oz) boneless skinless chicken breasts
1 tablespoon olive oil
1 yellow pepper
1 fresh green chilli
1 onion, chopped
50g (2oz) button mushrooms, sliced
2 teaspoons plain flour
200g (7oz) can chopped tomatoes
100ml (4fl oz) chicken stock
200g (7oz) can red kidney beans, drained
1 tablespoon tomato purée
1 teaspoon dried oregano
1–2 teaspoons chilli sauce
1 small ripe avocado
juice of ½ a lime
1 garlic clove, crushed
2 tablespoons Greek yogurt
1 spring onion
1 tablespoon chopped fresh coriander
75g (3oz) tortilla chips
50g (2oz) mature Cheddar cheese, grated
salt and freshly ground black pepper
sprigs of fresh coriander, to garnish

❶ Cut the chicken into 2.5cm (1in) chunks.

Heat the oil in a frying pan, add the chicken and fry for 3 minutes until browned.

❷ Meanwhile, cut the yellow pepper in half, remove the core and seeds and cut into bite-sized pieces. Cut the green chilli in half lengthways, remove the core and seeds and finely chop the flesh.

❸ Add the onion to the chicken and fry for 2 minutes. Add the yellow pepper, green chilli and mushrooms and fry for 2 minutes. Add the flour and cook for 1 minute, stirring. Stir in the chopped tomatoes and stock and bring to the boil, stirring. Add the kidney beans, tomato purée, oregano, chilli sauce, salt and pepper. Simmer for 5 minutes.

❹ Meanwhile, cut the avocado in half and remove the stone. Using a teaspoon, scoop the flesh into a bowl, keeping the halved shells. Add the lime juice, garlic, Greek yogurt, a little more chilli sauce, salt and pepper. Mash the avocado with a fork until smooth. Finely chop the spring onion and stir into the avocado mixture with the chopped coriander. Spoon the guacamole into a serving bowl. Spoon the chicken mixture into the halved avocado shells.

❺ Pre-heat the grill.

❻ Crunch the tortilla chips over the chicken. Sprinkle the Cheddar cheese over the tortilla chips and put under a pre-heated hot grill for about 2 minutes until the cheese has all melted.

7 Serve the Mexican chicken with the guacamole, garnished with sprigs of fresh coriander.

Sauté of Chicken with Cider and Caramelised Apples

SERVES 2

The combination of cider and apples is a true winner – add to this the succulent juiciness of chicken thighs and you have pure satisfaction. If you can only get chicken thighs with the bone in, cook for an extra 6–8 minutes.

1 potato, peeled
50g (2oz) butter
vegetable oil, for frying
4 boneless, skinless chicken thighs
1 shallot, chopped
1 garlic clove, crushed
100ml (4fl oz) dry cider
1 bouquet garni (see below)
1 Cox's apple
2 teaspoons sugar
100g (4oz) green beans, trimmed and halved
2 spring onions, trimmed
50ml (2fl oz) milk
a pinch of freshly grated nutmeg
salt and freshly ground black pepper
sprigs of fresh thyme, to garnish

Bouquet Garni *To make a bouquet garni, bunch together ½ a celery stick, 1 bay leaf, 1 fresh parsley stalk and 1 sprig of fresh thyme and tie together with a piece of string.*

1 Dice the potato and put into a saucepan of salted water. Bring to the boil then cook for 10 minutes.

2 Heat 15g (½oz) of butter and a little oil in a frying pan or wok. Season the chicken with salt and pepper and add to the pan. Add the shallot and garlic, season with salt and pepper and fry until browned.

3 Add the cider to the chicken, scraping any sediment from the bottom of the pan. Add the bouquet garni, bring to the boil, cover and simmer for 15 minutes until the chicken is tender.

4 Pre-heat the grill.

5 Peel the apple, quarter, remove the core and cut each quarter into 3 segments, making 12 slices in all. Melt the remaining butter then use some to brush over the apple slices. Sprinkle with sugar then grill to caramelise.

6 Put the beans into a pan of boiling salted water to cook for 4 minutes. Meanwhile, finely slice the spring onions.

7 Drain the potatoes and mash together with the remaining melted butter. Add the spring onions, reserving some to garnish, and just enough of the milk to achieve your required consistency of mashed potato. Season well with salt and pepper and add the nutmeg.

8 Drain the beans. Remove and discard the bouquet garni. Serve the chicken on top of the mashed potato, with the beans to one side, and the caramelised apple slices fanned around the chicken. Garnish with thyme sprigs and the reserved sliced spring onions.

Cannelloni Sorpresa

SERVES 2

Supermarkets have only recently started to display minced chicken, thanks to such programmes as Can't Cook Won't Cook. *Here's just one of its uses.*

4 sheets of dried lasagne
1 tablespoon sunflower oil
225g (8oz) stir-fry chicken pieces
4 tablespoons olive oil
1 small onion, chopped
1 large garlic clove, chopped
2 rashers of smoked streaky bacon
75g (3oz) button mushrooms, trimmed
a good splash of white wine
2 tablespoons tomato purée
¼ teaspoon dried sage
¼ teaspoon dried rosemary
a good pinch of freshly grated nutmeg
1 egg white
300ml (½ pint) carton cheese sauce
25g (1oz) freshly grated Parmesan cheese
3 handfuls baby spinach leaves
1 tablespoon white wine vinegar
salt and freshly ground black pepper

1 Put the sheets of pasta into a large saucepan of boiling salted water and add the vegetable oil. Turn off the heat and allow to stand for 5 minutes.

2 Meanwhile, put the chicken in a food processor and whizz until minced. Heat 1 tablespoon of the olive oil in a frying pan. Add the onion and garlic and fry until softened. Add the minced chicken and stir-fry until golden brown.

3 Meanwhile, cut the bacon into small strips and put in a small frying pan. Slice the mushrooms, add to the bacon and fry until golden brown.

4 Carefully lift the sheets of pasta out of the hot water and into a bowl of iced water.

5 Add a splash of wine to the chicken and cook for 30 seconds then add the tomato purée, sage, rosemary and nutmeg. Cook until the mixture is fairly dry. Season with salt and pepper.

6 Tip the chicken into a food processor, add the egg white and blend to a smooth purée. Add half the bacon and mushrooms, pulsating once or twice to mix but do not purée.

7 Pre-heat the grill.

8 Take a sheet of pasta and lay it on to a board. Spoon some of the chicken mixture on to one end of the pasta then roll up. Arrange the cannelloni in an ovenproof dish and scatter over the remaining bacon and mushroom mixture. Pour the cheese sauce on top and sprinkle over the Parmesan cheese. Grill until bubbling.

9 Whilst the cannelloni cook, wash and dry the spinach leaves, using a salad spinner. Make a quick oil and vinegar dressing by whisking the remaining olive oil, the vinegar, salt and pepper together. Toss the leaves in the dressing. Serve the cannelloni with the spinach salad.

Chinese Chicken with Egg-fried Rice

SERVES 4

Almost everyone loves Chinese food and this is a great all-in-one supper dish.

3 boneless, skinless chicken breasts
1 large garlic clove, chopped
2cm (¾in) piece of fresh root ginger, grated
3 tablespoons soy sauce
3 tablespoons teriyaki marinade or sauce
1 teaspoon honey
1 tablespoon sesame oil
2 medium carrots
8 spring onions
1 red pepper
100g (4oz) baby sweetcorn
3 tablespoons vegetable oil
100g (4oz) frozen peas
225g (8oz) long-grain rice, cooked
2 eggs, beaten
salt and freshly ground black pepper

1 Cut the chicken into thin strips.

2 Make a marinade by mixing together the garlic, ginger, soy sauce, teriyaki marinade, honey and sesame oil and stir into the chicken. Leave for at least 10 minutes whilst you prepare the vegetables.

3 Prepare the garnishes in advance. Pare the end of 1 carrot into a point. Then, using a small sharp knife, make small petal-like cuts around the carrot at the widest part of the point until the point comes away from the rest of the carrot, making a flower. Continue in this way to make flowers. Feather 3 of the spring onions by cutting the white part of the spring onion away from the green, then make fine cuts 2cm (¾ in) long at the cut end of the spring onion. Put into a bowl of cold water, place in the fridge and leave for 10 minutes until the ends curl.

4 Finely slice the remaining 5 spring onions, reserving half of the green slices for the egg-fried rice. Halve the red pepper, remove the core and seeds and slice the flesh. Slice the sweetcorn and the remaining carrot diagonally.

5 Heat 2 tablespoons of vegetable oil in a wok or large frying pan. When very hot add the spring onions, red pepper, sweetcorn, carrot and peas and stir-fry for 1–2 minutes. Tip out on to a plate.

6 Add the marinated chicken and the juices to the pan and stir-fry for 3 minutes.

Return the vegetables to the wok and stir-fry for a further minute.

7 Tip the stir-fry on to a serving dish and keep warm whilst you make the egg-fried rice. Heat the remaining oil in a frying pan and when hot add the cooked rice. When heated through make a well in the middle of the rice and pour in the beaten eggs. Scramble into the rice, season with salt and pepper and stir in the green ends of the spring onions.

8 Serve the rice around the chicken. Garnish with the carrot flowers and feathered spring onions.

MEAT DISHES

Beef in Black Bean Sauce *57*

Sausage Sizzlers *58*

Cabbage Parcels with Tomato Sauce *59*

Roast Beef and Yorkshire Pud *60*

Lamb and Pepper Kebabs with Creamy Haricot Beans *61*

Lattice Beef Wellington with Fondant Potatoes *62*

Chilli con Carne *63*

Speedy Moussaka *64*

Medallions of Pork in a Mushroom Sauce *65*

**Peppered Steak in a Creamy Sauce
with Caraway, Carrot and Cabbage** *66*

Breakfast in Bed *67*

Sherpa's Pie with Pea Masala *68*

Spiced Lamb Skewers with Tzatziki *69*

Beef Stroganoff *70*

Cheesy Hamburgers with Crunchy Relish *71*

Mango-glazed Lamb with Jewelled Couscous *72*

Lamb Meatballs with Couscous *73*

Fusilli Alla Carbonara with Herby Bread *74*

Feasta Meatza Pizza *75*

Beef in Black Bean Sauce

SERVES 2

Time to get the wok out and, believe me, it'll be worth it. Don't be put off if you can't get the water chestnuts — just leave them out.

2 tablespoons soy sauce
2 tablespoons dry sherry
1 teaspoon garlic purée
¼ teaspoon Chinese five spice powder
2cm (¾in) piece of fresh root ginger
275g (10oz) rump steak
2 spring onions
1 small onion
1 small red pepper
100g (4oz) thread egg noodles
1 tablespoon sunflower oil
1 tablespoon sesame oil
50g (2oz) unsalted cashew nuts
200g (7oz) can water chestnuts, drained
4 tablespoons black bean sauce

❶ Mix the soy sauce, sherry, garlic purée and five spice powder in a bowl. Peel then finely grate the ginger and add to the soy sauce mixture.

❷ Cut the beef into thin strips, add to the marinade, stir well and set aside to marinate.

❸ Cut off the roots and discard most of the tops from the spring onions. Cut 5cm (2in) pieces of spring onion. Slice lengthways into very thin strips, taking care not to cut all the way through. Put the spring onion brushes in a bowl of iced water for 10 minutes until curly. Finely slice the rest of the spring onions diagonally and set aside.

❹ Cut the onion in half then slice thinly. Cut the pepper in half and remove the core and seeds. Chop the pepper flesh into 2cm (¾in) diamonds.

❺ Add the thread noodles to a pan of boiling water, bring back to the boil and cook according to packet instructions.

❻ Heat the sunflower and sesame oil in a wok or large frying pan. Add the onion, pepper and cashew nuts and stir-fry for 1 minute. Add the marinated beef strips, reserving the marinade, and stir-fry for 3 minutes. Add the water chestnuts, black bean sauce, reserved marinade mixture and 4 tablespoons water and cook for 2 minutes.

❼ Add the reserved spring onions to the noodles. Drain the noodles and pile on to serving plates. Spoon over the beef in black bean sauce. Drain the spring onion brushes and scatter over the beef to garnish.

Marinating *The purpose of a marinade is to tenderise and add flavour to the meat so it is well worth doing if specified in a recipe, especially with tough cuts of meat. Some meats are left to marinate overnight or up to a day but most are left for about an hour.*

Sausage Sizzlers

SERVES 2

*A handy recipe that works surprisingly well as a starter
or for a casual supper party.*

1 garlic clove
5 tablespoons tomato ketchup
1 teaspoon Worcestershire sauce
1 teaspoon Dijon mustard
2 teaspoons clear honey
275g (10oz) good-quality pork sausagemeat
2 tablespoons chopped fresh herbs, such as parsley and chives
7 tablespoons olive oil
one 225g (8oz) potato, peeled
25g (1oz) unsalted butter
50g (2oz) mixed salad leaves (to include iceberg lettuce)
4 cherry tomatoes
2 spring onions
1 tablespoon white wine vinegar
salt and freshly ground black pepper

❶ To make the barbecue sauce, crush the garlic into a bowl and stir in the tomato ketchup, Worcestershire sauce, mustard and honey. Season with salt and pepper to taste.

❷ Put the sausagemeat in a bowl. Add 4 tablespoons of the barbecue sauce and half of the herbs and mix well. Divide the sausage mixture into 10 pieces then, with wetted hands, roll each piece into a ball then flatten slightly.

❸ Heat 2 tablespoons of the oil in a frying pan, then fry the sausage burgers for 6–8 minutes, turning occasionally until cooked through and golden.

❹ Bring a small saucepan of salted water to the boil and use the small end of a melon baller to make potato balls from the potato. Add to the pan, return to the boil and boil fast for 1 minute.

❺ Meanwhile, heat 1 tablespoon of the oil and the butter in a small frying pan. Drain the potatoes, season with salt and pepper and add to the frying pan. Fry gently for 3–4 minutes until tender and golden brown.

❻ To make the salad, break up the lettuce leaves into small pieces and arrange on serving plates. Cut the cherry tomatoes in half. Slice the spring onions diagonally. Scatter the tomatoes and onions on top of the lettuce.

❼ Place the remaining barbecue sauce and olive oil and the vinegar in a screw-topped jar and shake until well combined. Pour into a small pan and just heat through, adding a little water if necessary.

❽ Remove the potato balls from the pan, drain on kitchen paper then toss in the remaining herbs. Scatter the potato balls on the salad and drizzle some of the warm dressing on top. Serve at once with the sausage burgers.

Cabbage Parcels with Tomato Sauce

SERVES 2

Bring a touch of the Eastern European cuisine to your dining table with this simple succulent dish. Now, who's for a shot of vodka?

1 celery stick
1 garlic clove
1 onion
3 tablespoons olive oil
225g (8oz) minced pork
4 large Savoy cabbage leaves
25g (1oz) freshly grated Parmesan cheese
100g (4oz) cooked long-grain rice
1 teaspoon freeze-dried oregano
a pinch of freshly grated nutmeg
1 small courgette
1 teaspoon sugar
2 teaspoons cider vinegar
1 tablespoon sun-dried tomato purée
200g (7oz) can chopped tomatoes
salt and freshly ground black pepper
fresh chives, to garnish

1 Pre-heat the oven to 180°C/350°F/Gas 4.

2 Cut the celery stick lengthways into thin strips. Cut across the strips into fine dice. Crush the garlic clove. Finely chop the onion.

3 Heat 1 tablespoon olive oil in a saucepan. Add the diced celery, garlic and two-thirds of the onion and fry for 3 minutes. Add the minced pork and cook for 5 minutes.

4 Meanwhile, trim the stalks from the cabbage leaves. Blanch the cabbage leaves in a saucepan of boiling water for 3 minutes. Drain the cabbage leaves and refresh under cold running water.

5 Stir the Parmesan cheese, rice, oregano, nutmeg, salt and pepper into the pork. Spoon the pork filling into the centre of each cabbage leaf. Fold in the sides of the leaves, then roll up to enclose the filling completely. Place the cabbage parcels, seam side down, in a buttered ovenproof dish. Cover with foil and cook in the oven for 8 minutes.

6 Pre-heat a griddle pan or the grill. Slice the courgette diagonally. Brush the courgette with 1 tablespoon of olive oil and season well with salt and pepper. Cook in the griddle pan or under the hot grill for 5 minutes, turning once.

7 To make the sauce, heat the remaining olive oil in a saucepan, add the remaining onion and cook for 2 minutes. Add the sugar and vinegar. Stir in the sun-dried tomato purée, chopped tomatoes, salt and pepper. Simmer for 3 minutes. Using a hand-held blender, blend the sauce until smooth.

8 Put the cabbage parcels on serving plates, spoon over the tomato sauce and serve with the grilled courgettes. Garnish with chives.

Roast Beef and Yorkshire Pud

SERVES 2

A Sunday, or indeed midweek, roast that is quick and gives you perfect results. Once you've tried this easy recipe for cabbage, you won't want to go back to the ordinary boiled stuff.

3 tablespoons sunflower oil
225g (8oz) piece of beef fillet
1 teaspoon English mustard powder
50g (2oz) plain flour
1 egg
75ml (3fl oz) milk
1 tablespoon creamed horseradish
1 teaspoon sugar
1 lemon
75ml (3fl oz) double cream
225g (8oz) wedge of green cabbage
15g (½oz) butter, softened
½ teaspoon caraway seeds
salt and freshly ground black pepper

1 Pre-heat the oven to 220°C/425°F/ Gas 7. Generously brush half a mini muffin tray with about 2 tablespoons of the oil. Heat a small frying pan until very hot.

2 Season the beef with salt and pepper and rub in most of the mustard powder. Add the remaining oil to the pan and then brown the beef for 1 minute on each side. Transfer to a small roasting tin, and place on the middle shelf of the oven for 10 minutes. Place the prepared muffin tray on the top shelf of the oven.

3 Sift the flour into a bowl with a pinch of salt. Make a well in the centre and break in the egg. Add half the milk and beat until smooth. Then add the remaining milk, mixing until well combined.

4 Remove the muffin tray from the oven and divide the batter between the moulds. Cook in the oven for 10 minutes until well risen.

5 Mix together the remaining pinch of mustard, the horseradish and sugar. Grate in the rind of ½ the lemon and squeeze in 1 teaspoon of the juice. Whip the cream until it just holds its shape and then fold into the horseradish mixture. Set aside.

6 Remove the beef from the oven and leave to rest in a warm place.

7 Cut the cabbage in half, remove the central stalk and discard, then cut across the grain into 1cm (½in) slices. Put the butter and 1 tablespoon water in a frying pan, with a lid, over a high heat. Add the cabbage to the pan with the caraway seeds and a pinch of salt. Cover, shake and cook over a high heat for 1 minute. Shake again and cook for another 1 minute. Season with black pepper.

8 Carve the beef into thin slices and arrange on serving plates with some of the cabbage, horseradish cream and Yorkshire puddings. Serve at once.

Lamb and Pepper Kebabs with Creamy Haricot Beans

SERVES 2

As well as cooking these kebabs in a frying pan or under the grill, you can also barbecue them (weather permitting, of course). If you can't get haricot beans, use canellini or flageolet beans instead.

275g–350g (10–12oz) lamb fillet
4 tablespoons olive oil
1 large garlic clove
2 tablespoons chopped fresh parsley
1 teaspoon chopped fresh thyme
grated rind and juice of 1 lemon
1 red pepper
1 onion
3 rashers of smoked streaky bacon
1 red onion
450g can haricot beans, drained
75ml (3fl oz) double cream
salt and freshly ground black pepper
FOR THE GREEK SALAD
2 plum tomatoes
¼ cucumber
50g (2oz) feta cheese
3 tablespoons olive oil
1 tablespoon lemon juice

❶ Slice the lamb fillet into chunks. Make a marinade for the lamb by putting about 2 tablespoons of olive oil in a bowl. Crush the garlic and add to the oil with the chopped parsley, thyme, lemon rind and juice, salt and pepper. Turn the lamb in the mixture and leave in a cool place for up to 12 hours.

❷ Cut the red pepper in half, remove the core and the seeds and then cut the flesh into chunks, the same size as the lamb chunks. Cut the onion into the same size chunks. Thread the pepper, onion and lamb chunnks alternately on to metal skewers or soaked wooden skewers.

❸ Heat 1 tablespoon of oil in a shallow frying pan or pre-heat the grill. When hot, add the kebabs and cook for 6–8 minutes, turning occasionally.

❹ Meanwhile, finely slice the streaky bacon and the red onion. Heat the remaining olive oil in a saucepan, add the sliced bacon and onion and fry until just crisp. Stir in the beans and any leftover marinade from the lamb and cook for 4 minutes. Stir in the cream and check the seasoning.

❺ Make the salad by dicing the plum tomatoes, the cucumber and the feta cheese. Whisk together the oil and lemon juice and season with salt and pepper. Pour over the salad ingredients and toss together.

❻ Serve the kebabs with the beans and Greek salad.

Lattice Beef Wellington with Fondant Potatoes

SERVES 2

When a food item, such as ready-rolled herbed lattice puff pastry,
that saves time in the kitchen comes along, I always try to use it on the show.

2 teaspoons vegetable oil
two 100g (4oz) fillet steaks
2 medium baking potatoes
50g (2oz) butter
300ml (½ pint) chicken stock
1 bay leaf
2 tablespoons medium-coarse mushroom pâté
2 sheets frozen ready-rolled herbed lattice puff pastry
1 egg, beaten
150g (5oz) baby Brussels sprouts
salt and freshly ground black pepper
FOR THE RED WINE SAUCE
100ml (4fl oz) red wine
4 teaspoons redcurrant jelly
½ a chicken stock cube, crumbled
salt and freshly ground black pepper

❶ Pre-heat the oven to 230°C/450°F/ Gas 8.

❷ Heat the oil in a frying pan and when very hot, brown the steaks quickly on all sides to seal in the juices. Lift on to a plate and leave to cool.

❸ Cut the potatoes into large chunks, leaving the skin on. Put into a deep frying pan with the butter, stock and bay leaf and cover with a circle of greaseproof paper, so the potatoes steam while they cook. Leave to simmer gently until tender. If liked, brown under a hot grill.

❹ Season the steaks with salt and pepper and spread generously with pâté. Place each steak, pâté side down, on the pastry sheets. Brush the edges with the beaten egg and wrap up the steaks, covering completely. Carefully turn over and place on a baking tray. Brush with the remaining egg and bake in the oven for 12 minutes or until the pastry is golden brown.

❺ Meanwhile, make the sauce. Add the wine to the pan you browned the steaks in and bring to the boil. Stir in the redcurrant jelly and the stock cube then ladle in some of the buttery liquid from the potatoes. Season with salt and pepper and cook over a gentle heat, whisking from time to time. Add a little hot water if necessary.

❻ Bring a pan of salted water to the boil for the Brussels sprouts. Trim the ends of the sprouts and cut a cross on the stumps. Cook for 3–4 minutes until tender then drain.

❼ To serve, place the steaks on serving plates, spoon over some of the sauce and add the fondant potatoes and sprouts.

Chilli con Carne

SERVES 2

This classic dish needs no introduction. Suffice to say it's a delicious recipe and made the way chilli should be. If you like your food spicy, add another teaspoon (or more) of chilli powder.

1 large onion
1 red pepper
15g (½oz) butter
2 tablespoons sunflower oil
100g (4oz) long-grain rice
1 garlic clove
1 teaspoon chilli powder
1 teaspoon ground cumin
275g (10oz) lean minced beef
2 teaspoons plain flour
200g (7oz) can chopped tomatoes
150ml (¼ pint) beef stock
4 tablespoons red wine
200g (7oz) can red kidney beans, drained
1 tablespoon tomato purée
1 teaspoon dried oregano
2 spring onions
6 tablespoons soured cream
salt and freshly ground black pepper

❶ Chop the onion. Cut the red pepper in half and discard the core and seeds. Finely dice one quarter of the pepper and roughly chop the rest.

❷ Melt the butter and 1 tablespoon oil in a saucepan. Add one-third of the onion and cook for 2 minutes. Stir in the rice and the diced red pepper. Add 300ml (½ pint) boiling water, return to the boil, cover and simmer for 10 minutes until the rice is tender and the liquid has been absorbed.

❸ Heat 1 tablespoon of oil in a pan, add the rest of the onion and cook for 3 minutes. Crush the garlic and add to the onion with the chopped red pepper. Cook for 2 minutes. Sprinkle in the chilli powder and cumin. Stir in the minced beef and cook for 2 minutes. Stir in the flour and cook for 1 minute. Add the chopped tomatoes, stock and red wine and bring to the boil, stirring. Stir in the kidney beans, tomato purée, oregano, salt and pepper and simmer for 5 minutes.

❹ Finely slice the spring onions. Mix three-quarters of the spring onions with the soured cream and season with salt and pepper.

❺ Lightly oil 2 ramekin dishes. Spoon the cooked rice into the dishes and press down with the back of a spoon. Place a serving plate on top of each dish and quickly turn both over together. Slide the dish on each plate so it is to one side, then lift the dish off the rice.

❻ Spoon the chilli con carne next to the rice. Put a spoonful of the spring onion and soured cream mixture next to the chilli. Scatter the reserved spring onion slices over the soured cream.

Speedy Moussaka

SERVES 2–4

Forget those greasy experiences you sometimes associate with moussaka and holidays in Greece. This is a great recipe that tastes even better the following day.

1 onion
about 4 tablespoons olive oil
2 garlic cloves
350g (12oz) lean minced lamb
1 large potato, weighing about 225g (8oz)
1 small aubergine, weighing about 350g (12oz)
½ teaspoon ground cinnamon
1 teaspoon dried oregano
50ml (2fl oz) red wine (optional)
200g (7oz) can chopped tomatoes
2 tablespoons tomato purée
about 150ml (¼ pint) vegetable stock
75g (3oz) Cheddar cheese
25g (1oz) butter, softened
2 tablespoons plain flour
350ml (12fl oz) milk
1 baby cucumber
4 small ripe tomatoes
a handful of pitted black olives
½ a lemon
salt and freshly ground black pepper
flat-leaved parsley sprigs, to garnish

❶ Finely chop the onion. Heat 1 tablespoon of the oil in a frying pan, add the onion, reserving 1 tablespoon, and fry until softened. Crush in the garlic and add the lamb, stirring now and then until browned.

❷ Meanwhile, cut the potato into thin slices and add to a saucepan of boiling water. Cover and cook for 6–8 minutes until tender.

❸ Pre-heat a frying pan. Cut the aubergine lengthways into slices and brush both sides with a little of the oil and season well with salt and pepper. Cook in the frying pan for 2–3 minutes on each side until lightly golden and cooked through.

❹ Stir the cinnamon and half of the oregano into the lamb and cook for about 30 seconds. Add the wine, if using, the can of tomatoes, tomato purée and enough of the stock to make a thick sauce. Reduce the heat and simmer for about 5 minutes until tender and well reduced.

❺ Grate the cheese. Melt the butter in a small pan and stir in the flour. Cook for a couple of minutes, then gradually whisk in the milk until completely smooth. Add half of the cheese and season to taste with salt and pepper.

❻ Pre-heat the grill.

❼ Drain the potatoes and put in an ovenproof dish. Spoon over the lamb mixture and arrange the aubergine on top. Pour over the sauce. Sprinkle over the remaining cheese and grill until bubbling.

8 Cut the cucumber into quarters, remove the seeds and slice diagonally. Cut 1 tomato into quarters and remove the seeds. Cut thin slices, not quite to the top of each quarter, and prise open into a fan. Chop the remaining tomatoes and place in a bowl. Cut the olives in half and add to the tomatoes, reserving a couple to garnish. Add the reserved onion and remaining oregano. Squeeze over the lemon and a drizzle of oil. Season with salt and pepper and toss well together. Serve the salad with the moussaka, garnished with a parsley sprig, tomato fan and a couple of olives.

Medallions of Pork in a Mushroom Sauce

SERVES 2

When buying pork, look for a light pink colour. Medallions are a little more expensive as they come from the fillet, but they're well worth the extra pennies. For a posh dinner party, use wild or oyster mushrooms instead of button.

225g (8oz) pork tenderloin
1 large potato
1 tablespoon paprika
2 shallots
100g (4oz) closed-cup mushrooms
2 tablespoons olive oil
15g (½oz) butter
50ml (2fl oz) chicken stock
grated rind and juice of ½ a lemon
2 tablespoons crème fraîche
8 cherry tomatoes, stalks left on
salt and freshly ground black pepper
a few sprigs of rosemary, to garnish

1 Slice the pork into 2cm (¾ in) thick pieces. Place between 2 sheets of polythene and, using a mallet or rolling pin, flatten into 1cm (½ in) thick rounds.

2 Peel then grate the potato over a tea-towel. Season with salt and pepper and half the paprika. Gather up the edges of the tea-towel and wring the excess liquid from the potato. Finely chop the shallots. Slice the mushrooms.

3 Heat 1 tablespoon of oil and the butter in a frying pan. In the middle of the pan, carefully shape the grated potato into 2 pancake shapes. If you have a metal ring use it to shape the rösti. Fry gently and turn over when golden brown. Take care that the potato doesn't burn.

4 In another frying pan, heat the remaining oil. Add the medallions of pork and fry gently for 3–4 minutes on each side. When cooked remove the pork from the pan and keep warm whilst you make the sauce.

5 If necessary, add a drop more oil to the pan. Add the chopped shallots and fry for 1 minute then add the sliced mushrooms and cook until soft. Stir in the remaining paprika. Add the stock to the pan, scraping any meat juices from the bottom of the pan, and bring to the boil. Add the lemon rind and juice, remove from the heat and stir in the crème fraîche. Add salt and pepper to taste, if necessary.

6 Add the tomatoes to the pan the rösti cooked in and fry briefly to warm through.

7 To serve, put a rösti on each serving plate. Arrange the medallions on top and spoon over the sauce. Serve the tomatoes on one side and garnish with rosemary.

Peppered Steak in a Creamy Sauce with Caraway, Carrot and Cabbage

SERVES 2

If you're feeling fancy, you could use fillet steak instead. If you haven't got brandy, use sherry or try it with apple juice or diluted lemon juice.

2 tablespoons green peppercorns
two 175–225g (6–8oz) sirloin or rump steaks
¼ medium cabbage
2 large carrots
2 tablespoons sunflower oil
25g (1oz) butter
2 teaspoons caraway seeds
1 tablespoon chopped fresh parsley
1 egg cup of brandy
100ml (4fl oz) double cream
salt and freshly ground black pepper

1 Put the peppercorns under a tea-towel or polythene and, using a rolling pin, mallet or heavy-based saucepan, crush well. Gently press into both sides of the steaks.

2 Finely shred the cabbage and then grate the carrots. Set them to one side.

3 Divide the oil and the butter between 2 frying pans and heat. Add the steaks to 1 and the cabbage to the other. Fry the steaks for 2 minutes on each side if you like them medium cooked and 3 minutes on each side for well done. When the steaks are cooked, remove and keep warm.

4 Add the grated carrots to the cabbage and stir-fry until the cabbage is tender. The vegetables should still have a bite to them when done. Add the caraway seeds and season with salt and pepper. Stir in the chopped parsley.

5 To make the sauce, add the brandy to the pan that the steaks were cooked in and set it alight to flambé. Add the cream and season sparingly with salt.

6 To serve, pour the sauce over the steaks and spoon the cabbage and carrot on one side.

Serving Suggestion *Peppered steak needs simply to be served with boiled new potatoes.*

Breakfast in Bed

SERVES 2

Chance would be a fine thing if, like me, you have young kids. For a special day, this fry-up makes a perfect start.

2 slices of bread
225g (8oz) sausagemeat
1 tablespoon chopped fresh parsley
1 teaspoon chopped fresh thyme
a splash of Worcestershire sauce
1 tablespoon plain flour
olive oil, for frying
25g (1oz) butter
4 rashers of rindless back bacon
2 eggs
8 button mushrooms
4 cherry tomatoes
salt and freshly ground black pepper

1 Using a 7.5cm (3in) plain cutter, cut rounds from the centre of each slice of bread. Toast the rounds and keep the leftover frames for later.

2 Using a fork, mash the sausagemeat with the parsley, thyme, Worcestershire sauce, salt and pepper. Flour your hands and shape the sausagemeat into 4 patties. Heat about 2 tablespoons of oil and half the butter in a large frying pan and gently fry the patties for 3 minutes on each side.

3 Trim the bacon and fry with the patties, turning halfway through cooking.

4 Heat another frying pan and add the remaining butter and about 2 tablespoons of oil. Put the leftover frames of bread into the pan, cook for 30 seconds then turn over. Break an egg into the hole and fry for 2 minutes. Season with salt and pepper. If you like the top of your egg well set, pre-heat the grill, and put the frying pan with the framed eggs under the grill to finish cooking for 1 minute.

5 Remove the patties and bacon from the pan and drain on kitchen paper. Fry the mushrooms and tomatoes in the frying pan.

6 Put the toast on serving plates and place the sausage patties on top. Serve with the framed eggs, mushrooms and tomatoes.

Serving Suggestion *To complete the Breakfast in Bed treat, serve on a tray with some freshly squeezed orange juice and hot coffee.*

Sherpa's Pie with Pea Masala

SERVES 2

During the days of the Raj in India, the Brits would get their cooks to prepare traditional home cooking, such as shepherd's pie, but add their own herbs and spices to give the dish a bit of body. This is how Sherpa's pie was born.

350g (12oz) potatoes
1 onion
1 large plum tomato
a little sunflower oil
1cm (½in) cube of fresh root ginger, peeled
1 large fresh green chilli
225g (8oz) lean minced lamb
1 teaspoon garam masala
1 teaspoon tomato purée
1 tablespoon tamarind (see below)
about 150ml (¼ pint) lamb stock
a small bunch of fresh coriander
50g (2oz) butter
50ml (2fl oz) milk
½ a lemon
1 egg yolk
1 teaspoon cumin seeds
1 garlic clove
75g (3oz) frozen peas, thawed
75g (3oz) frozen sweetcorn, thawed
salt and freshly ground black pepper

❶ Peel the potatoes and cut into small dice. Cook in a covered saucepan of salted boiling water for 8 minutes until tender.

❷ Meanwhile, finely chop the onion. Put the tomato in a bowl, cover with boiling water for 30 seconds then plunge into iced water. Using a sharp knife, peel off the skin then finely chop the flesh, discarding the seeds.

❸ Heat a little oil in a frying pan, add half of the onion and fry until lightly golden. Grate the ginger and finely chop the chilli, discarding the pith and seeds. Add half the chilli and all the ginger to the pan and fry for 1 minute, stirring. Add the lamb and cook, stirring, for 2–3 minutes until browned. Add half of the garam masala, half the tomato purée, the tamarind, chopped tomato and enough stock to make a sauce. Season with salt and pepper and cook for 5 minutes.

❹ Melt 40g (1½oz) of the butter in a small pan and fry the remaining chilli for 10 seconds. Set aside. Finely chop the coriander.

❺ Drain the potatoes and mash until smooth. Beat in the coriander, chilli butter mixture, milk, a squeeze of lemon, salt and pepper. Spoon the mixture into a piping bag. Pour the lamb into an ovenproof dish and pipe the potato on top.

Tamarind This dark-brown sticky pulp comes from the large seed pod of the Indian tamarind tree. It has a fruity, sour taste and is much used in Indian cooking. Ready-to-use pulp is available in jars.

6 Pre-heat the grill. Mix the egg yolk with a little water and brush over the piped potato. Grill for about 3–4 minutes until golden.

7 Heat the remaining butter in a wok. Stir-fry the cumin seeds for 10 seconds, add the remaining onion, garam masala and tomato purée and cook for 1 minute. Crush the garlic and add to the pan with the peas and sweetcorn and toss until heated through.

8 Spoon the pea masala on to serving plates, add a squeeze of lemon and serve with the pie.

Spiced Lamb Skewers with Tzatziki

SERVES 2

This is the type of meal that transports you back to one of your favourite holiday destinations at any time of the year.

1 small onion
a selection of fresh herbs, including parsley, mint, chives and oregano
225g (8oz) lean minced lamb
¼ teaspoon ground coriander
¼ teaspoon mixed spice
¼ teaspoon chilli powder
¼ teaspoon ground cumin
a little olive oil
10cm (4in) piece of cucumber
150ml (5fl oz) natural yogurt
2 garlic cloves
2 small plum tomatoes
50g (2oz) block of feta cheese
a handful of small black olives
1 lemon, halved
25g (1oz) butter
4 small white pitta breads
salt and freshly ground black pepper

1 Roughly chop the onion and put in the food processor. Add a small bunch of the herbs and whizz until finely chopped. Add the lamb, coriander, mixed spice, chilli powder, cumin and plenty of salt and pepper and whizz to form a paste.

2 Take the mixture out of the food processor and divide it into 4 portions. With wetted hands, roll each into a sausage shape about 10cm (4in) long.

3 Heat a griddle pan or large frying pan. Thread each sausage shape on to a soaked wooden skewer (see page 70) that is about 15cm (6in) long.

4 Brush the pan with a little oil and cook the skewers for 6–8 minutes, turning occasionally, until cooked through but still moist.

5 Meanwhile, make the tzatziki. Cut the piece of cucumber into quarters, remove the seeds, and then cut into small dice.

Stir into the yogurt and season with salt and pepper. Crush ½ a garlic clove and cut some mint leaves into ribbons. Add both to the yogurt mixture, stirring to combine.

6 Cut the tomatoes into wedges and arrange on serving plates. Crumble the feta and sprinkle on top of the tomatoes with the olives. Drizzle over a little oil and add a squeeze of lemon. Season with pepper. Chop some parsley and scatter on top.

7 Melt the butter. Finely chop the remaining garlic and stir into the melted butter. Chop some of the herbs and add to the butter. Grill the pitta breads until toasted on one side. Spoon the butter on to the uncooked side of the pitta. Grill until sizzling and then cut into fingers.

8 Arrange the skewers on the serving plates with a good spoonful of the tzatziki and some pitta fingers. Add a lemon wedge and serve.

....

Wooden Skewers *When using wooden skewers, soak them in water for 30 minutes before use as this helps to stop the food from sticking to them.*

Beef Stroganoff

SERVES 2

This classic dish is usually served with rice but goes equally well with noodles. For an extra sharp taste, add a couple of tablespoons of white wine vinegar with the apple juice.

100g (4oz) egg and spinach noodles
350g (12oz) beef rump steak
2 tablespoons plain flour
1 tablespoon paprika
1 onion
25g (1oz) butter
1 tablespoon sunflower oil
100g (4oz) button mushrooms
1 glass of apple juice, about 100ml (4fl oz)
1 small courgette
½ red pepper
150ml (¼ pint) soured cream
salt and freshly ground black pepper
chopped fresh parsley, to garnish

1 Add the noodles to a saucepan of boiling water and cook for 8 minutes until just tender.

2 Slice the beef into 1 x 5cm (½ x 2in) strips. Season the flour with salt, pepper and paprika. Add the strips of beef and toss to coat in the seasoned flour.

3 Slice the onion. Melt 15g (½oz) butter and the oil in a frying pan. Add the onion and cook for 3 minutes. Meanwhile, wipe and slice the mushrooms. Add the strips of beef to the onion and cook, stirring frequently, for 3 minutes. Stir in the sliced mushrooms and cook for 3 minutes. Then add the apple juice. Stir then simmer gently.

④ Trim the ends off the courgette, then cut into 4cm (1½ in) lengths. Cut each piece into matchsticks. Slice the pepper flesh into matchsticks, discarding the seeds. Drain the noodles and leave in the colander, covered with a lid.

⑤ Melt 15g (½ oz) butter in the pan used to cook the noodles. Add the courgette strips, red pepper, salt and pepper and cook for 3 minutes. Add the noodles and toss together.

⑥ Stir the soured cream into the beef and cook gently for 1 minute, without boiling.

⑦ Spoon the beef stroganoff on to serving plates and serve with the noodles. Garnish with parsley.

Cheesy Hamburgers with Crunchy Relish

SERVES 2

This one's a real winner with the kids. For a change, why not try using chicken or turkey mince, which are also widely available from supermarkets?

1 baked potato
olive oil
225g (8oz) lean minced beef
a pinch of dried mixed herbs
1 egg yolk
25g (1oz) Cheddar cheese
2 hamburger buns
salt and freshly ground black pepper
a few lettuce leaves, to garnish
a few slices of onion, to garnish
1 tomato, sliced, to garnish
FOR THE RELISH:
1 small can sweetcorn
2 tablespoons white wine vinegar
1 spring onion, finely sliced
1–2 teaspoons sugar
¼ red pepper, finely diced (optional)

① Pre-heat the grill. To make the potato skins, cut the potato into wedges, drizzle with olive oil and place under the grill until golden and crisp.

② Mix together the beef, mixed herbs, egg yolk, salt and pepper. Form the mixture into 4 patties. Grate the cheese. Sandwich the cheese between 2 patties and press around the edge to seal.

③ Heat a little oil in a frying pan. Add the patties and fry for 3–4 minutes on each side.

④ To make the relish, put all the ingredients in a saucepan, bring to the boil and simmer for 5 minutes. Season with salt and pepper.

⑤ To serve, place the hamburgers in a bun. Garnish with lettuce, slices of onion and tomato. Serve with the potato skins and a little of the corn relish.

Mango-glazed Lamb with Jewelled Couscous

SERVES 2

Sometimes a name itself can be a great inspiration, and if you add colour and texture you have the perfect combination to get those eyes going wide in anticipation and mouth juices flowing.

225ml (8fl oz) vegetable stock
3 tablespoons hot mango chutney
4 tablespoons tikka paste
1 teaspoon paprika
25g (1oz) raisins
100g (4oz) pre-cooked couscous
350g (12oz) lamb steaks
3 tablespoons natural yogurt
1 teaspoon finely chopped garlic
1 teaspoon finely chopped ginger
25g (1oz) butter
5cm (2in) piece of cucumber
1 small red apple
2 tablespoons chopped fresh coriander
1 tablespoon sunflower oil
2 extra-large poppadoms
salt and freshly ground black pepper
lemon slices, to garnish

Couscous *Couscous is produced by moistening grains of semolina which are then formed into tiny pellets and coated with wheat flour. It is cooked by steaming it but pre-cooked couscous is available in packets from supermarkets.*

❶ Pre-heat the oven to 200°C/400°F/Gas 6 and pre-heat the grill.

❷ Pour the stock into a small heavy-based saucepan and add 1 tablespoon of the chutney, 1 teaspoon of the tikka paste, the paprika and raisins and bring to the boil.

❸ Remove the pan from the heat and pour in the couscous, stirring continuously. Leave to swell for 2 minutes.

❹ Cut the lamb into 2.5cm (1in) pieces. Mix together the yogurt, garlic, ginger and the remaining tikka paste and add the lamb, stirring until well coated.

❺ Add the butter to the couscous mixture, and return to a very gentle heat. Cook for 3 minutes, stirring with a fork to separate the grains. Remove the pan from the heat and cover.

❻ Thread the lamb on to soaked bamboo skewers and grill on a foil-lined grill rack for about 10 minutes, turning occasionally.

❼ Meanwhile, cut the piece of cucumber in half, remove the seeds and dice the flesh. Core the apple and cut into dice. Add the cucumber, apple, coriander, salt and pepper to the couscous and stir together until well mixed.

❽ Brush the poppadoms with the oil and

place in the oven for 2–3 minutes until puffed up and golden. Drain on kitchen paper.

9 Brush the remaining mango chutney all over the skewers. Place the poppadoms on serving plates and heap the jewelled couscous on top. Arrange the skewers at the side, garnish with the lemon slices and serve at once.

Lamb Meatballs with Couscous

SERVES 2

Gone are the days when it took hours to prepare couscous: now it's simple to cook and is a good alternative to rice, pasta or potatoes. If you can't get hold of harissa, replace it with a teaspoon of Tabasco sauce.

1 onion
1 courgette
3 tablespoons olive oil
100g (4oz) couscous
250ml (8fl oz) vegetable stock
half a 400g (14oz) can chick-peas, drained
1 cinnamon stick
25g (1oz) no-soak dried apricots
1 slice of bread, crusts removed
225g (8oz) lean minced lamb
2 teaspoons ground coriander
2 teaspoons ground cumin
a few drops of Tabasco or hot chilli sauce
2 tablespoons chopped fresh parsley
2 tomatoes
1 garlic clove
4 tablespoons white wine
1 teaspoon harissa (see right)
150ml (¼ pint) creamed tomatoes
salt and freshly ground pepper
sprigs of flat-leaved parsley, to garnish

1 Very finely chop the onion. Cut the courgette into quarters lengthways then cut into 1cm (½in) dice. Heat 1 tablespoon of olive oil in a saucepan. Add half of the onion and cook for 2 minutes. Add the courgette and cook for 2 minutes. Add the couscous, stock, chick-peas, cinnamon stick, salt and pepper. Chop the apricots and add to the pan. Cover and cook gently for 3 minutes.

2 Put the bread in a bowl and cover with cold water. Drain, squeeze out the excess water and return to the bowl. Add the rest of the onion, minced lamb, coriander, cumin, Tabasco sauce, half the parsley, salt and pepper and, using your hands, mix well together. Shape the mixture into golf-sized balls.

3 Put the tomatoes in a bowl, cover with boiling water for about 30 seconds then

Harissa *This is a hot mixture of chilli and up to 20 spices and is available in powder and paste form. Use the canned paste variety in this recipe.*

plunge into iced water. Using a sharp knife, peel off the skins then dice the flesh, discarding the seeds. Crush the garlic.

❹ Heat the remaining olive oil in a frying pan. Add the meatballs and cook for 5 minutes, turning frequently. Lift the meatballs out of the frying pan and drain on absorbent kitchen paper. Set aside and keep hot.

❺ Add the wine, tomatoes, garlic and harissa to the frying pan and cook for 2 minutes. Stir in the creamed tomatoes, remaining chopped parsley, salt and pepper. Bring to the boil and simmer for 2 minutes.

❻ Fluff up the couscous with a fork and spoon on to serving plates. Pile the meatballs on top. Drizzle the tomato sauce over the meatballs and garnish with sprigs of parsley.

Fusilli alla Carbonara with Herby Bread
SERVES 2

Parsley is so much more than just a garnishing herb — it's full of nutrients such as vitamins A, B and C, iron and calcium. Use it liberally in this recipe.

200g (7oz) fusilli (spiral-shaped pasta)
50g (2oz) Parmesan cheese
40g (1½oz) butter, softened
1 teaspoon Dijon mustard
1 large garlic clove, crushed
3 tablespoons chopped fresh mixed herbs, such as parsley and chives
1 small French stick
4 rindless unsmoked streaky bacon rashers
1 small onion
4 tablespoons olive oil
2 eggs
2 tablespoons single cream
75g (3oz) mixed salad leaves
a squeeze of lemon juice
salt and freshly ground black pepper
shavings of Parmesan cheese, to garnish

❶ Pre-heat the oven to 200°C/400°F/Gas 6.

❷ Put the pasta in a large saucepan of boiling salted water and cook for 8–10 minutes until just tender.

❸ Grate the Parmesan cheese and put 2 tablespoons in a bowl. Add the butter, mustard, half the garlic, half the herbs, salt and pepper and mix together.

❹ Slice the French stick diagonally, almost but not completely through. Spread with the butter and wrap in a piece of foil. Place on a baking tray and bake for about 10 minutes until heated through.

❺ Place the bacon rashers on top of each other and cut into thin strips. Finely chop the onion. Heat 2 tablespoons of the oil in a frying pan. Add the onion to the pan and fry for 2 minutes until softened. Stir in the remaining garlic then add the bacon and fry over a high heat for 2 minutes.

6 Put the remaining Parmesan cheese and herbs in a bowl with the eggs and cream and season with salt and pepper to taste. Beat lightly with a balloon whisk.

7 Drain the pasta and return to the pan with the bacon and onion mixture. Stir over a moderate heat for 1 minute until combined. Remove the pan from the heat and stir in the egg mixture. Leave in the pan for 1–2 minutes and the heat will cook the egg to a sauce.

8 Tear the salad leaves into bite-sized pieces and drizzle over the remaining oil and lemon juice. Season with salt and pepper and toss to dress.

9 Turn the pasta on to serving plates and garnish with Parmesan shavings. Add some salad and herby bread and serve at once.

....

Parmesan Shavings *To make shavings of Parmesan cheese, using a potato peeler with a U-shaped handle and swivel blade, shred long shavings from a rectangular piece of cheese.*

Feasta Meatza Pizza

SERVES 2

Here's a dish that'll save on the phone bill, cut down on pollution, save the batteries on your doorbell and won't rip the bin bags with hard-to-get-rid-of boxes.

1 tablespoon sunflower oil
225g (8oz) lean minced lamb
1 garlic clove
2 tablespoons tomato purée
200g (7oz) can chopped tomatoes
a good pinch of dried oregano
50g (2oz) mushrooms
1 small red onion
75g (3oz) Cheddar cheese
75g (3oz) mozzarella cheese
18cm (9in) thin-crust pizza base
salt and freshly ground black pepper
1 tablespoon chopped fresh herbs, such as chives and parsley, to garnish

1 Pre-heat the oven to 220°C/425°F/Gas 7.

2 Heat the oil in a frying pan and fry the mince for 2–3 minutes until browned, stirring.

3 Crush the garlic and add to the pan with the tomato purée, chopped tomatoes, oregano, salt and pepper. Cook for another 3–4 minutes until thickened, stirring.

4 Meanwhile, slice the mushrooms and then slice the onion, separating each slice into rings. Grate the Cheddar and mozzarella cheese.

5 Place the pizza base on a baking tray and spoon over the mince. Scatter the mushrooms and onion rings on top and sprinkle over the cheese. Bake for 10 minutes until bubbling and golden. Sprinkle with the herbs and serve cut into slices.

DESSERTS

Apple and Pear Crumble with Fresh Custard Sauce 77

Swiss Chocolate Cherry Roll 78

Fudgy Chocolate Puddings 79

Star-spangled Raspberry Soufflés 80

Spiced Red Wine Pear Cobbler 81

Christmas Chocolate and Chestnut Roulade 82

Mango and Coconut Fool with Brandy Snaps 83

Mango and Banana Brûlée 84

Tiramisu 84

Minted Shortcake with Summer Fruits 85

**Mini Muffins with
Instant Ice-cream** 86

Blueberry Pancake Towers 87

Triple Tipple Trifle 88

Tarte Tatin and Berry Custard 89

**Apple Stars with
Brandy Fudge Sauce** 90

Peach Melba Meringue Roulade 91

Summer Berry Crisp 92

Sweet Soufflé Omelette 93

Baked Alaska and Strawberry Compote 94

Apple and Pear Crumble with Fresh Custard Sauce

SERVES 4

It's hard to resist a good crumble, especially when that extra crunchiness comes in the form of hazelnuts, so have a go. You might need to make more custard if, like me, you're very fond of it.

FOR THE CRUMBLE
2 eating apples
2 small pears
15g (½oz) stem ginger
2 tablespoons ginger syrup from the jar of stem ginger
100g (4oz) plain flour
50g (2oz) butter
50g (2oz) chopped hazelnuts
½ teaspoon ground cinnamon
75g (3oz) demerara sugar
FOR THE CUSTARD SAUCE
300ml (½ pint) milk
2 teaspoons cornflour
2 egg yolks
1 tablespoon caster sugar
a few drops of vanilla extract

1 Pre-heat the oven to 220°C/425°F/Gas 7.

2 Core and slice the apples. Put in a saucepan with 2 tablespoons water and cook gently.

3 Meanwhile, quarter the pears, remove the cores and cut into 1cm (½in) thick slices. Finely chop the stem ginger. Add the pears, chopped ginger, and ginger syrup to the pan, cover and cook for 5 minutes.

4 Meanwhile, sift the plain flour in a food processor. Dice the butter, add to the flour and process until the mixture looks like fine breadcrumbs. Add the chopped hazelnuts, cinnamon and ⅔ of the demerara sugar.

5 Spoon the pear and apple mixture into an ovenproof dish. Spread the hazelnut crumble over the fruit. Sprinkle the rest of the demerara sugar on top of the crumble. Bake in the oven for 10–12 minutes until the top is golden.

6 Meanwhile, make the custard sauce. Put the milk in a saucepan, reserving 3 tablespoons, and heat to just below boiling point. In a bowl, mix the cornflour with a little water to form a smooth paste. Add the egg yolks, caster sugar and the rest of the milk and beat together until smooth. Pour the hot milk on to the egg mixture, whisking all the time. Strain back into the pan and cook, whisking, until slightly thickened. Stir in the vanilla extract.

7 Serve the apple and pear crumble with the custard sauce.

Swiss Chocolate Cherry Roll

SERVES 6

This easy-to-prepare dessert reminds me of the classic Black Forest gâteau, but is much simpler to make. Use good, plain chocolate with at least 65% cocoa solids for a rich chocolatey taste.

a little melted butter, for greasing
50g (2oz) plain flour, plus extra for dusting
50g (2oz) caster sugar, plus extra for dusting
2 eggs
a pinch of salt
2 teaspoons cocoa powder
75g (3oz) plain chocolate
225ml (8fl oz) double cream
425g (15oz) can pitted black cherries, drained and halved
6 physalis (see below)
3 tablespoons raspberry jam

1 Pre-heat the oven to 190°C/375°F/ Gas 5. Brush a Swiss roll tin with melted butter and line the bottom with greaseproof paper. Brush again with melted butter and dust with flour and sugar.

2 Break the eggs into a large bowl and add the sugar. Using an electric whisk, whisk until pale, thick and fluffy. Sift the flour, salt and cocoa into the eggs, and add 1 tablespoon warm water. Using a metal spoon, gently fold into the eggs. Pour into the lined tin, smooth to the edges and bake for 8–10 minutes.

3 Meanwhile, break the chocolate into a bowl placed over a saucepan of simmering water, and heat gently until melted. Remove from the heat.

4 Whip the cream until stiff and add 1 tablespoon of the melted chocolate to marble the cream. Fold in the cherry halves.

5 Remove the papery skin from the physalis then dip the berries into the melted chocolate and leave to cool on greaseproof paper.

6 Spread a clean tea-towel on to the work surface and sprinkle with caster sugar. When the Swiss roll is cooked, turn it out on to the sugared surface and peel off the greaseproof paper. Trim the edges with a knife. Leave to cool.

7 When the Swiss roll is cool, spread it with the raspberry jam and then with the whipped cream mixture. Using the cloth to help you, roll up the cake firmly from one end. Drizzle the remaining chocolate on top of the Swiss roll and decorate with the chocolate-covered fruit.

Physalis *These are also known as Cape gooseberries and are small, golden berries encased in a papery skin. They have a scented, delicate flavour, similar to that of a gooseberry.*

Fudgy Chocolate Puddings

SERVES 4

These are just so gooey, they're divine.

50g (2oz) plain chocolate
50g (2oz) unsalted butter, plus extra for greasing
25g (1oz) caster sugar
25g (1oz) walnuts
1 egg
15g (½oz) self-raising flour
6 tablespoons single cream
3 tablespoons golden syrup
1 tablespoon cocoa powder
1–2 tablespoons brandy
icing sugar, to dust
orange shreds, to decorate (see below)
mint sprigs, to decorate

1 Pre-heat the oven to 220°C/425°F/ Gas 7. Butter four 100ml (4fl oz) ramekin dishes.

2 Break the chocolate into pieces and put in a small heavy-based saucepan. Add half the butter and heat gently, stirring, until the chocolate has completely melted. Stir the caster sugar and 3 tablespoons hot water into the chocolate mixture and continue stirring until the sugar has dissolved. Leave to cool.

3 Place a roasting tin in the pre-heated oven and pour in enough hot water to come 1cm (½ in) up the sides. Carefully slide back in the oven shelf.

4 Finely chop the walnuts. Separate the egg into 2 separate clean bowls. Whisk the egg white until it holds its shape. Stir the egg yolk and nuts into the chocolate mixture and fold in the flour. Finally fold in the egg white and divide the mixture between the ramekin dishes. Stand in the roasting tin and bake for about 10 minutes until firm to the touch.

5 Meanwhile, put the remaining butter, half the cream and golden syrup in a small pan. Sift in the cocoa powder then heat gently. Slowly bring to the boil, stirring occasionally. Flavour with the brandy and simmer for a further 2–3 minutes. Remove from the heat and leave to cool.

6 Flood the serving plates with some of the sauce. Place small blobs of the remaining cream around the edge and gently pull a cocktail stick through to make small heart shapes. Run a knife around the edge of the puddings and turn out on to the plates. Dust with icing sugar and decorate with the orange shreds and mint sprigs. Serve at once.

* * *

Orange Shreds *You can make orange shreds in one of two ways. Run a canelle knife over the surface of an orange and then cut the peel into thin slices or do the same with a zester, which removes the outer peel in shreds.*

Star-spangled Raspberry Soufflés

SERVES 4

I'm a great fan of raspberries in case you haven't noticed. They're quite cheap in season, from June to October in Britain. The imported ones can be expensive, especially out of season and if you buy the yellow or white varieties.

25g (1oz) unsalted butter, plus extra for greasing

175g (6oz) caster sugar, plus extra for dusting

a little sunflower oil, for brushing

25g (1oz) plain flour

100ml (4fl oz) milk

2 eggs

a few drops of vanilla extract

100g (4oz) raspberries

50g (2oz) crème fraîche or Greek yogurt

a few mint sprigs, to decorate

icing sugar, to dust

❶ Pre-heat the oven to 220°C/425°F/Gas 7. Grease 4 ramekin dishes, measuring about 7.5cm (3in) in diameter and 5cm (2in) high, with butter and dust with caster sugar. Cover a baking tray with a piece of foil, smoothing it down. Brush with a little oil.

❷ Melt the 25g (1oz) butter in a small heavy-based saucepan, stir in the flour and cook for 1 minute. Gradually stir in the milk, a little at a time, until combined. Remove from the heat and stir in 25g (1oz) of the sugar.

❸ Separate the eggs and place the egg whites in a clean grease-free bowl. Stir the egg yolks and vanilla extract into the sauce until smooth.

❹ Whisk the egg whites until they just hold their shape in soft peaks then whisk in 25g (1oz) of the sugar. Continue to whisk until slightly thicker then fold in 25g (1oz) sugar. Using a large metal spoon, mix a quarter of the meringue into the white sauce and then carefully fold in the rest.

❺ Reserve some raspberries for decoration then mash the rest with 25g (1oz) of the sugar. Divide between the prepared ramekin dishes.

❻ Pour the soufflé mixture on top and place on a baking tray. Using the tip of a knife, release the mixture from the edge of the dishes and bake for 8–10 minutes until well risen and lightly golden.

❼ Meanwhile, put the remaining sugar in a small heavy-based pan with 1 tablespoon water. Heat gently until the sugar dissolves then boil fast until golden brown. Using a metal spoon, drizzle the caramel in criss-cross patterns on to the foil-lined baking tray. Leave to set.

❽ Place small dollops of crème fraîche or

yogurt around serving plates and decorate with the reserved raspberries and mint sprigs. Stick a piece of caramel into the centre of each mound of crème fraîche. Place the raspberry soufflés on the plates, dust with icing sugar and serve at once.

Spiced Red Wine Pear Cobbler

SERVES 2

Pears are an incredibly versatile fruit. Serve them on their own with cheese, such as Pecorino or Parmesan, or with soft green peppercorns for a deliciously hot aromatic dessert.

100g (4oz) self-raising flour
½ teaspoon baking powder
pinch of salt
25g (1oz) butter
3 tablespoons caster sugar
50ml (2fl oz) milk
150ml (¼ pint) red wine
½ teaspoon ground cinnamon
a pinch of freshly grated nutmeg
a pinch of ground cloves
2 tablespoons redcurrant jelly
1 lemon
2 firm dessert pears
75ml (3fl oz) double cream
2 tablespoons Greek yogurt
1 tablespoon icing sugar
mint sprigs, to decorate

1 Pre-heat the oven to 230°C/450°F/Gas 8.

2 Sift the flour, baking powder and salt into a bowl. Dice the butter then add to the flour and, using your fingertips, rub until the mixture looks like fine breadcrumbs. Stir in 1 tablespoon caster sugar. Make a well in the centre of the dry ingredients.

Stir in the milk and mix to form a fairly soft dough. You may need to add more flour if it's too sticky.

3 Lightly dust the work surface with flour. Turn the dough out on to the work surface and knead very gently until smooth. Shape the dough into a 1cm (½ in) thick circle. Using a 7.5cm (3in) plain cutter, cut out 2 circles.

4 Put on a baking tray and brush with a little milk. Sprinkle 1 tablespoon of sugar over them. Bake in the oven for 8 minutes until well risen and golden.

5 Meanwhile, put the red wine, the remaining 1 tablespoon of caster sugar, the cinnamon, nutmeg, cloves and redcurrant jelly in a saucepan. Using a zester, remove strips of rind from half the lemon and add to the pan. Heat gently.

6 Peel and core the pears. Cut into thick slices. Add the sliced pears to the spiced red wine mixture and bring to the boil. Cover the pan and simmer for 5 minutes.

7 Put the cream in a bowl and whip until it just holds its shape. Fold in the Greek yogurt and icing sugar.

8 Using a slotted spoon, remove the cooked pear slices from the spiced red wine mixture.

9 Return the spiced red wine to the heat and boil rapidly for 2 minutes until syrupy.

10 Put the cobblers on serving plates, arrange the pear slices on top and spoon the syrup over the pears. Spoon some of the cream into the centre and decorate with mint sprigs.

Christmas Chocolate and Chestnut Roulade

SERVES 4–6

A great alternative to your average Christmas log, and the chestnut parcel mixed with cream is simply to die for.

3 eggs
150g (6oz) caster sugar
50g (2oz) plain flour
25g (1oz) cocoa powder
450ml (¾ pint) double cream
½ teaspoon vanilla extract
50g (2oz) plain chocolate
50g (2oz) chestnut purée
25g (1oz) green ready-to-roll icing
25g (1oz) red ready-to-roll icing
icing sugar, for dusting

1 Pre-heat the oven to 200°C/400°F/ Gas 6. Grease and line a 30.5 x 20.5cm (12 x 8in) Swiss roll tin.

2 Using an electric whisk, whisk the eggs and 100g (4oz) sugar together until thick and pale. Sift in the flour and cocoa and carefully fold in, then fold in 1 tablespoon hot water. Pour into the prepared tin and bake for 8–10 minutes until risen and firm to the touch.

3 Meanwhile, make the filling. Rinse the whisks then whip the cream until it holds its shape. Add the vanilla extract and 25g (1oz) of the sugar, then whip until stiff. Spoon a third of the cream into a piping bag fitted with a 1cm (½in) nozzle. Set aside. Finely chop or grate the chocolate and add to the remaining whipped cream then add the chestnut purée and stir together.

4 Roll out the green icing and cut out holly leaves, either with a cutter or freehand. Roll the red icing into small balls to form holly berries. Set aside.

5 Place a clean damp tea-towel on to a work surface. Cover with greaseproof paper and sprinkle with the remaining caster sugar. Take the roulade out of the oven. Tip over on to the greaseproof paper and carefully peel off the lining. Trim the edges and leave to cool.

6 Spread the chestnut cream over the

roulade. Carefully roll up and place on to a serving plate. If the roulade cracks, don't worry. Dust liberally with icing sugar.

7 Pipe the cream down the centre of the roulade and decorate with the holly leaves and berries.

Mango and Coconut Fool with Brandy Snaps

SERVES 4–6

Brandy snaps always look impressive, and yet they're so easy to make. Clean rubber gloves will help when it comes to shaping them while they're still hot.

50g (2oz) sugar
50g (2oz) butter
2 tablespoons golden syrup
50g (2oz) plain flour
a pinch of ground ginger
3 ripe mangoes
25g (1oz) caster sugar
juice of 1 lime
300ml (½ pint) double cream
200ml (7fl oz) canned coconut milk
coconut shavings, to decorate

1 Pre-heat the oven to 190°C/375°F/Gas 5.

2 Put the sugar, butter and golden syrup in a saucepan and heat gently until melted. Remove from the heat and stir in the flour and ginger.

3 Put teaspoons of the mixture well apart on baking trays. Bake in the oven for 5 minutes. When golden, remove from the oven. Whilst they start to cool (45 seconds–1 minute) clear the table surface and get a rolling pin, palette knife and wire cooling tray ready. Make the brandy snaps by rolling them around the rolling pin, then cooling them on the wire rack. You will need to work fast or the biscuits will harden before you have a chance to roll them. If this happens, return the brandy snaps to the oven to soften them.

4 Stand a mango on a board on its long rounded edge. Cut a thick slice down either side of the mango, keeping the knife as close to the stone as possible. Scrape the flesh out of the skin and put in a food processor. Repeat with a second mango. Add the caster sugar and the lime juice and whiz up to make a rough purée.

5 Whip the cream until stiff. Mix in the coconut milk and mango purée. Put the fool in a serving bowl and chill.

6 Slice 2 cheeks off the remaining mango and cut into slices. Decorate the fool with shavings of coconut fanned out in the centre and slices of mango around the outside. Serve with the brandy snaps.

Mango and Banana Brûlée

SERVES 2

A perfectly simple dessert that always get a nod of approval around the dinner table. Use fresh mangoes by all means (and suck on the stones when no one's looking!).

1 small banana
400g (14oz) can mango slices in syrup, drained
3 tablespoons Greek strained yogurt
1 tablespoon lime juice
3 tablespoons sugar

1 Pre-heat the grill to very hot.

2 Roughly slice the banana and put in a bowl. Add the mango slices, yogurt, lime juice and 1 tablespoon of the sugar. Blend together until smooth.

3 Spoon the mixture into 2 flameproof, glass ramekin dishes. Top with the remaining sugar. (This will partially dissolve to form a light crust.)

4 Place the dishes under the grill and cook until bubbling. Allow to cool slightly before serving.

Tiramisu

SERVES 4

Yes, it's creamy and rich but, once you've tried it, tiramisu is hard to resist. If you like a boozy taste, drizzle over 3–4 tablespoons of Marsala wine or sweet sherry on to the sponges. Very naughty, but so nice.

2 eggs
3 tablespoons caster sugar
225g (8oz) mascarpone cream cheese
100g (4oz) plain chocolate
1 teaspoon instant coffee
4 tablespoons coffee liqueur
100g (4oz) sponge finger biscuits
1 tablespoon cocoa powder
6 physalis (cape gooseberries) or orange slices, to decorate

1 Separate the eggs into 2 clean bowls. Add the caster sugar to the yolks and whisk together until pale and creamy. Add the mascarpone cheese to the egg yolk mixture and beat until smooth and fluffy. Chop 50g (2oz) of the chocolate and stir into the mascarpone mixture.

2 Whisk the egg whites until stiff. Carefully fold into the mascarpone mixture.

3 Dissolve the coffee in 2 tablespoons

boiling water. Mix in the liqueur and 100ml (4fl oz) cold water. Dip the sponge finger biscuits into the coffee mixture, one at a time, and use to line the bottom of a serving dish.

4 Spread a layer of the mascarpone mixture over the soaked biscuits. Repeat the layers of soaked biscuits and mascarpone mixture once more.

5 Using a vegetable peeler, shave down the edge of the remaining chocolate, to make chocolate curls.

6 Place the chocolate curls on top of the tiramisu and dust lightly with the cocoa powder. If using, peel back the papery skin from the physalis and twist. Decorate the tiramisu with the twists or orange slices.

Minted Shortcake with Summer Fruits

SERVES 4

A beautiful combination of fine-flavoured fruits means that desserts such as this one can be prepared all summer long in a matter of minutes.

75g (3oz) butter, softened

40g (1½oz) caster sugar

75g (3oz) plain flour, plus extra for dusting

25g (1oz) cornflour

2 teaspoons chopped fresh mint

175g (6oz) strawberries

1–2 teaspoons icing sugar, plus extra for dusting

dash of kirsch (optional)

350g (12oz) mixed summer fruits, such as redcurrants, raspberries, strawberries, mango and kiwi fruit

150ml (¼ pint) double cream

mint sprigs, to decorate

---

1 Pre-heat the oven to 200°C/400°F/Gas 6. Line a baking tray with parchment paper.

2 Cream the butter and sugar together in a bowl until pale and fluffy. Sift in the flour and cornflour and blend together. Add the mint and beat with a wooden spoon until the dough comes together.

3 On a lightly floured surface, cut the dough in half and roll out thinly. Using a fluted cutter, stamp out four 7.5cm (3in) rounds. Repeat with the remaining dough.

4 Arrange the rounds on the baking tray and bake in the oven for about 6 minutes until golden brown.

5 Meanwhile, hull the strawberries and put in a food processor. Blend until smooth then add icing sugar to taste and a dash of kirsch, if using.

⑥ Prepare your selection of fruit for the filling and cut into bite-sized pieces, if necessary.

⑦ Remove the shortbread biscuits from the oven and, using a palette knife, transfer to a wire rack.

⑧ In a bowl, whip the cream until stiff. Place 1 shortbread round on each serving plate and cover with the cream. Arrange some of the fruit on top and top with another shortbread round. Decorate with a little more fruit, such as a sprig of redcurrants, and spoon around some of the strawberry coulis. Dust the whole of the plates with icing sugar, decorate with mint sprigs and serve at once.

Mini Muffins with Instant Ice-cream

SERVES 4

So simple, this treat is child's play. In fact when I made this recipe with the kids during the holidays it was an immediate success with children right across Britain. So do try it, I'm sure you'll become a muffin lover instantly.

25g (1oz) butter, plus extra for greasing
a little sunflower oil, for brushing
50ml (2fl oz) milk
1 egg, beaten
a few drops of vanilla extract
50g (2oz) white chocolate
75g (3oz) self-raising flour
a pinch of salt
½ teaspoon baking powder
25g (1oz) light muscovado sugar
2 tablespoons demerara sugar
15g (½oz) macadamia nuts
225ml (8fl oz) double cream
2 tablespoons icing sugar, plus extra for dusting
300g (11oz) frozen raspberries
mint sprigs, to decorate

① Pre-heat the oven to 200°C/400°F/Gas 6. Butter a 12 hole mini muffin tin generously with butter. Line a baking tray with foil and brush with oil.

② Melt the 25g (1oz) butter. Pour the milk into a bowl and whisk in the egg, butter and vanilla extract.

③ Chop the chocolate. Sift the flour, salt and baking powder into a bowl and stir in the muscovado sugar. Using a metal spoon, lightly fold in the milk mixture, taking care not to over-mix. Stir in the chocolate and spoon the mixture into the muffin tin. Sprinkle over a little of the demerara sugar and bake for about 10 minutes until well risen and firm.

④ Roughly chop the nuts. Place the remaining demerara sugar in a small saucepan with 1 tablespoon water and cook gently until the sugar dissolves. Stir in the nuts and, once the mixture has become caramelised, pour out on to the baking tray. Leave to cool a little.

5 Meanwhile, put the cream, icing sugar and the frozen raspberries, reserving a few for decoration, into a food processor or blender and whiz on a low speed until well blended.

6 Break the nut mixture into pieces. Shape the ice-cream into scoops and place on serving plates. Sprinkle over some of the nut mixture and add muffins to each plate. Decorate with the reserved raspberries and a mint sprig. Dust with icing sugar and serve.

Blueberry Pancake Towers
SERVES 4

Blueberries, the dusty, blue-coloured fruit that are round with a slightly flattened top and bottom, are ideal for quick desserts as there's no labour involved. Although they're nice to eat raw, they come into their own when cooked.

150g (5oz) self-raising flour
¼ teaspoon ground cinnamon
3 tablespoons caster sugar
50g (2oz) butter
1 egg
225ml (8fl oz) milk
175g (6oz) small blueberries
2 large bananas
juice of ½ a lemon
25g (1oz) chopped nuts
227g (8oz) carton of crème fraîche
about 4 tablespoons maple syrup
mint sprigs, to decorate
icing sugar, to dust

1 Pre-heat the oven to 150°C/300°F/Gas 2 and pre-heat the grill. Heat a flat griddle pan.

2 Sift the flour, cinnamon and 1 tablespoon of the sugar into a bowl. Melt the butter and allow to cool.

3 Separate the egg by putting the egg white in a clean grease-free bowl, and the yolk in a jug. Add half of the butter and the milk to the yolk and whisk together.

4 Make a well in the centre of the flour and gradually add the liquid to make a smooth batter.

5 Whisk the egg white until stiff and carefully fold into the batter. Then stir in 100g (4oz) of the blueberries.

6 Brush the griddle pan with a little butter and ladle on spoonfuls of the batter, allowing them to spread to about 7.5cm (3in). Reduce the heat and cook for about 1½ minutes until small bubbles appear on the surface. Turn over and cook for another 1–2 minutes until lightly browned. Stack on a plate and keep warm in the oven. Repeat to make 12 pancakes.

7 Heat a small frying pan. Slice the

bananas and toss in the remaining butter and the lemon juice. Arrange on a baking tray, place on the grill pan and sprinkle a little of the remaining sugar over each. Grill under a high heat until caramelised and golden brown.

❽ Meanwhile, put the nuts in the small frying pan and cook until toasted, tossing frequently.

❾ Remove the pancakes from the oven and layer up 3 for each serving with the banana slices and a spoonful of crème fraîche.

Drizzle with maple syrup and a sprinkling of nuts as you go. Top with a quenelle of crème fraîche, scatter over the remaining blueberries and decorate with a mint sprig. Dust with icing sugar and serve at once.

Quenelle Shapes *To make a quenelle of crème fraîche, with two dessertspoons, take a scoop of crème fraîche, shape into an oval with one spoon and use the other to gently push it off on to the pancakes.*

Triple Tipple Trifle
SERVES 4–6

A real favourite of mine that's also proved to be a big hit with the viewers. I always use free-range eggs for this recipe to give a depth of flavour. Young children and pregnant women should give this one a miss as it contains raw eggs.

1 packet of trifle sponges
2 tablespoons raspberry jam
450g (1lb) can raspberries in syrup
50g (2oz) macaroons or Amaretti biscuits
50g (2oz) flaked almonds
100ml (4fl oz) dessert wine
3 large bananas
3 eggs
100g (4oz) caster sugar
225g (8oz) mascarpone cream cheese
1 small orange or satsuma
1 chocolate flake
glacé cherries, to decorate

❶ Slice the trifle sponges in half width-ways and sandwich together with the jam. Put in the bottom of a serving bowl. Add the raspberries with their juice. Crush the macaroons in your hands and sprinkle on top. Add half the almonds and pour over the dessert wine. Peel the bananas, slice and add to the bowl.

❷ Put the remaining almonds in a dry frying

Whisking Egg Whites *The important rule when whisking egg whites is to put them into a clean, dry, grease-free bowl, making sure that there is no egg yolk in them. This will ensure that you will achieve a good volume when whisked.*

pan and heat, tossing frequently, until golden.

③ Separate the eggs, putting the whites in a clean bowl and the yolks in another. Whisk the egg whites until fairly stiff, then add half the caster sugar and whisk again until stiff. Add the rest of the sugar to the egg yolks and beat until thick and pale then stir in the mascarpone cheese.

④ Using a large metal spoon, fold the egg whites into the mascarpone mixture and spoon on to the trifle.

⑤ Thinly slice the orange or segment the satsuma. Crumble the chocolate over the top of the trifle, add a few toasted almonds and decorate with the glacé cherries and the orange or satsuma.

Tarte Tatin and Berry Custard

SERVES 3–4

Tarte Tatin is a classic French dessert: upside-down apple tart. This is a really easy version; the custard contains lightly cooked eggs, so children and pregnant women should avoid it.

3 medium to large Cox's apples
25g (2oz) unsalted butter
5 tablespoons caster sugar
a pinch of ground cinnamon
1 sheet of ready-rolled puff pastry
450g (1lb) bag frozen summer fruits, thawed
300ml (½ pint) milk
2 egg yolks

① Pre-heat the oven to 240°C/475°F/Gas 9.

② Peel, core and slice the apples. Melt the butter in a large frying pan, add the apples, 3 tablespoons caster sugar and the cinnamon and caramelise, stirring frequently.

③ Using an ovenproof pie plate as a template, cut a circle out of the pastry. Arrange the caramelised apple slices in the middle of the plate and cover with the pastry circle. Place on a baking tray and bake in the oven for 10 minutes or until the pastry has puffed up and turned golden brown.

④ Meanwhile, push half of the fruit through a fine sieve to make a purée. Stir in 1 tablespoon sugar, to taste.

⑤ Heat the milk and the remaining sugar in a saucepan and bring to just below boiling point. Put the egg yolks in a bowl and pour over the milk, whisking continuously. Pour the mixture back into the pan and stir, over a gentle heat, until the custard has thickened. Just before serving, swirl in the remaining fruits to create a ripple effect.

⑥ Take the tart out of the oven, invert on to a serving plate and serve with the berry custard.

Apple Stars with Brandy Fudge Sauce

SERVES 2

This never fails to impress and it tastes absolutely scrummy. You might want to mark the star shape on the pastry before you cut it out to make it easier, or go for a simpler shape instead such as a triangle or a circle.

2 tablespoons apricot jam
juice of ½ a lemon
250g (9oz) ready-rolled puff pastry
1 red eating apple
2 glacé cherries (optional)
50g (2oz) granulated sugar
175ml (6fl oz) double cream
1 tablespoon brandy
1 tablespoon golden syrup
FOR THE COMPOTE
2 Cox's apples
2 satsumas
25g (1oz) butter
25g (1oz) brown sugar
25g (1oz) sultanas
1 teaspoon ground cinnamon
½ teaspoon ground mixed spice
2 cloves

1 Pre-heat the oven to 220°C/425°F/ Gas 7.

2 Put the apricot jam and lemon juice in a saucepan and heat gently to form a glaze.

3 Put the pastry on a lightly floured surface and cut out 2 star shapes.

4 Core and slice the red apple and arrange the slices, overlapping, in the centre of the stars. Decorate with the glacé cherries. Using a pastry brush, glaze with the melted apricot jam.

5 Bake in the oven for 8–10 minutes until golden brown.

6 Meanwhile, make the compote. Peel, core and chop the 2 Cox's apples. Then peel and segment the satsumas. Melt the butter in a saucepan and stir in the chopped apple, satsumas, brown sugar, sultanas, ground cinnamon, mixed spice and cloves and cook gently until the apples are soft.

7 To make the sauce, in another saucepan mix together the sugar, double cream, brandy and golden syrup. Stir until the sugar dissolves and the sauce boils and thickens.

8 Pour the sauce on to serving plates and tip the plates up so that the sauce covers the bottom.

9 Place the star tarts on the sauce and serve with the apple compote.

Peach Melba Meringue Roulade

SERVES 4–6

As with prawn cocktail, some people turn up their noses at the mention of peach melba, but both dishes are superb when done properly. Always use ripe peaches to allow the sweetness and flavour of the fruit to come through.

2 large egg whites
75g (3oz) caster sugar, plus extra for sprinkling
½ teaspoon cornflour
¼ teaspoon white wine vinegar
1 large ripe peach
300ml (½ pint) double cream
2 tablespoons Cointreau or Grand Marnier liqueur
100g (4oz) raspberries
mint sprigs, to decorate

1 Pre-heat the oven to 200°C/400°F/ Gas 6. Lightly grease and line a 23 x 30.5cm (9 x 12in) Swiss roll tin with non-stick parchment paper.

2 Put the egg whites in a bowl and whisk until stiff and dry. Add half the sugar and whisk until shiny then gradually whisk in the remaining sugar. Gently fold in the cornflour and vinegar. Using a spatula, spread the mixture into the prepared Swiss roll tin. Bake in the oven for 12 minutes until golden brown and cooked through. Remove from the tin by lifting the lining

paper and leave to cool on a wire rack.

3 Meanwhile, plunge the peach into a saucepan of boiling water for about 30 seconds then remove with a slotted spoon. Peel, halve and cut 5 large slices from the peach and set aside. Finely chop the remaining flesh.

4 Pour the cream into a bowl and whip until stiff then fold in the liqueur. Spoon about 5 tablespoons into a piping bag, fitted with a large star nozzle. Alternatively, the cream can be swirled on by hand, to decorate. Fold the finely chopped peach into the remaining cream mixture.

5 Place a large piece of parchment paper on the work surface and sprinkle over a little caster sugar. Turn the meringue on to the paper and carefully peel away the parchment lining. Spread over the cream mixture and sprinkle most of the raspberries on top, reserving 5 for decoration.

6 Roll up the roulade and pipe or swirl the remaining cream on top. Decorate with the reserved peach slices and raspberries and mint sprigs. Cut into slices and serve at once.

Summer Berry Crisp

SERVES 2

Glazed fruits need a bit of care and attention, so make sure you are completely ready before beginning the dipping stage of this recipe. Use the fruits within a few hours or the glaze will start to weep.

25g (1oz) rolled oats
2 tablespoons demerara sugar
25g (1oz) flaked almonds
2 tablespoons runny honey
50g (2oz) caster sugar
225g (8oz) mixed summer berries
150ml (¼ pint) double cream
4 tablespoons crème fraîche
mint sprigs, to decorate

1 Pre-heat the oven to 200°C/400°F/ Gas 6. Lightly grease a Swiss roll tin. Cover a baking tray with foil and lightly grease.

2 Put the oats, demerara sugar, almonds and honey in a bowl and mix well together. Spread the mixture on to the Swiss roll tin. Bake in the oven for 5 minutes.

3 Meanwhile, put the caster sugar in a small heavy-based saucepan with 3 table- spoons of water. Cook over a low heat until the sugar has completely dissolved. Increase the heat of the sugar syrup and boil fast until pale golden, brushing down the sides of the pan occasionally with a pastry brush, dipped in some water. Remove from the heat and leave to cool slightly for 1–2 minutes.

4 Remove the oat mixture from the oven, give it a good stir then return to the oven for another 5 minutes until crisp and golden. Tip the oat mixture out on to a large plate, spread out and leave until cool enough to handle.

5 Meanwhile, select some berries for decoration and dip into the caramel, holding the fruit on a cocktail stick or bamboo skewer and turning to coat. Place on the prepared tray and set aside to harden.

6 Whip the double cream until it just holds its shape and then fold in the crème fraîche.

7 Lightly crush the remaining berries with a fork and place in the bottom of two large, tall dessert glasses.

8 Using your fingers, break up the oat mixture to make small clusters (this helps it to cool down quicker and become crunchy). Sprinkle a layer of the oat mixture on top of the berries and spoon over some of the cream mixture. Continue layering, finishing with the cream mixture. Decorate with the caramel fruits and mint sprigs and serve.

Sweet Soufflé Omelette

SERVES 2

The secret of a good soufflé omelette is heat control. If the heat's too high, the light mixture will burn. Check the colour while the omelette is cooking by using a palette knife to lift up the edge carefully.

2 tablespoons sultanas
3 tablespoons dark rum
2 eggs and 1 egg yolk
3 tablespoons icing sugar
50g (2oz) butter
2 small bananas
1 teaspoon ground mixed spice
1 orange
2 tablespoons apricot jam
icing sugar, to dredge
mint or rosemary sprigs, to decorate

1 Put the sultanas in a bowl, add the rum and leave to soak.

2 Separate the eggs into 2 clean bowls. Whisk the egg whites with 1 tablespoon of the icing sugar until they hold their shape. Whisk the 3 egg yolks with the remaining icing sugar until pale and thick. Using a large metal spoon, fold the whites carefully into the yolks.

3 Melt half the butter in a non-stick frying pan, add the egg mixture and cook over a very low heat.

4 Meanwhile, cut the bananas into 1cm (½ in) slices. Melt the remaining butter in a frying pan and when hot, add the bananas with the mixed spice. Add the grated orange rind, the soaked sultanas and the rum and flambé the fruits. Stir in the apricot jam.

5 Pre-heat the grill then cook the omelette under a hot grill for 2 minutes until lightly brown.

6 Meanwhile, peel and segment the orange. Heat a metal skewer in a naked flame.

7 Remove the omelette from the grill and put the fruit mixture on one half. Carefully fold over and tip out on to a serving plate. Dredge the omelette with icing sugar and make a pattern on the omelette with the hot skewer. Decorate with mint or rosemary sprigs and the orange segments.

Baked Alaska and Strawberry Compote

SERVES 6–8

The availability of fresh strawberries is such that this dish can be made any time of the year. English strawberries are good in season, otherwise go for the Spanish ones. Try this with different flavours of ice-cream, such as Neapolitan.

450g (1lb) strawberries
450g (1lb) frozen raspberries
grated rind of 1 orange
225g (8oz) caster sugar
50ml (2fl oz) sweet wine or orange juice
4 egg whites
20.5–23cm (8–9in) flan case
1 litre (1¾ pints) vanilla ice-cream
25g (1oz) butter

❶ Pre-heat the oven to 230°C/450°F/Gas 8.

❷ Hull and quarter the strawberries. Mix the raspberries, orange rind and 25g (1oz) of the sugar and sprinkle with the wine or orange juice.

❸ To make the meringue, put the egg whites in a clean grease-free bowl and, using a hand-held electric whisk, whisk the whites until stiff. When stiff, fold in 175g (6oz) of the sugar, in stages, and whisk again until stiff.

❹ Put three-quarters of the raspberries on to the flan. Run a knife around the ice-cream, turn on to the raspberries and squash into a good shape. Fill a piping bag, fitted with a large star nozzle, with the meringue and pipe over the ice-cream to completely cover.

❺ Bake in the oven for 5 minutes.

❻ Meanwhile, make the strawberry compote. Melt the butter in a saucepan. Add the strawberries, remaining raspberries and the marinade and the remaining 25g (1oz) sugar and cook gently. Serve with the baked alaska.

The Meringue Test *After whisking, to test if your egg whites are stiff enough, hold the bowl, upside down – if they stay in the bowl they are the correct texture.*

Index

Apple
  and Pear Crumble with Custard Sauce 77
  Caramelised Apple with Sauté of Chicken and Cider 52–3
  Stars with Brandy Fudge Sauce 90
Aubergine Stacks with Caesar Salad 32–3
Avocado and Smoked Salmon Tagliatelle 28–9

Baked Alaska and Strawberry Compote 94
Banana, and Mango Brûlée 84
Beef
  Chilli con Carne
  in Black Bean Sauce 57
  Lattice Beef Wellington with Fondant Potatoes 62
  Peppered Steak in a Creamy Sauce with Caraway,
    Carrot and Cabbage 66–7
  Roast Beef and Yorkshire Pud 60
  Stroganoff 70–1
Blueberry Pancake Towers 87–8
Brandy
  Fudge Sauce 90
  Snaps 83
Breakfast in Bed 67

Cabbage Parcels with Tomato Sauce 59
Caesar Salad 32–3, 49
Cannelloni Sorpresa 53–4
Cheese
  Cheesy Hamburgers with Crunchy Relish 71
  Soufflés with Stilton Sauce and Tomato Bites 14–15
Chicken
  and Port Christmas Crackers 40
  Calabrian Chicken Bake 38
  Chinese Chicken with Egg-fried Rice 54–5
  Jambalaya with Tropical Fruit Skewers 37–8
  Jerk Chicken with Rice 'n' Peas 42
  Lemon Chicken and Asparagus Pasta 44
  Mexican Chicken with Guacamole 51–2
  Red Hot Drumsticks with Sweetcorn Skewers 39
  Sauté of Chicken with Cider and Caramelised Apples 52–3
  Shredded Sesame Chicken 48–9
  Thai Curry Chicken 46
  Viceroy's Creamy Curry Chicken 50
  Wholemeal Pancakes with Ricotta 49
Chocolate
  Christmas Chocolate and Chestnut Roulade 82–3
  Fudgy Puddings 79
  Swiss Chocolate Cherry Roll 78
Chow Mein, New Year 41
Coconut, and Mango Fool 83
Cod, Sweet and Sour Nuggets 34–5
Coleslaw, Christmas 13–14
Couscous
  Jewelled Couscous with Mango-glazed Lamb 73–4
  with Lamb Meatballs 7
Curry
  Fruit and Vegetable 18–19
  Goan Fish with Spicy Vegetables 23
  Thai Chicken 46
  Viceroy's Creamy Chicken 50
Custard 77
  Berry 89

Duck, Peking 45

Fish see also individual headings
  Cakes, Smoked with Vegetable Ribbons 29
  Curry, Goan 23
  Pie 27–8
  Spiced with Tabbouleh 33–4
Frittata, Zorba's 15–16
Fusilli alla Carbonara with Herby Bread 74–5

Hamburgers, Cheesy with Crunchy Relish 71
Harissa 73

Jambalaya with Tropical Fruit Skewers 37–8

L

Lamb
and Pepper Kebabs with Creamy Haricot Beans 61
Mango-glazed Lamb with Jewelled Couscous 72–3
Meatballs with Couscous 73–4
Spiced Lamb Skewers with Tzatziki 69–70
Lentils, Hot and Sour 31

M

Mango
and Banana Brûlée 84
and Coconut Fool with Brandy Snaps 83
-glazed Lamb with Jewelled Couscous 72–3
Marinating 57
Minted Shortcake with Summer Fruits 85–6
Moussaka, Speedy 64–5
Muffins, Mini with Instant Ice-cream 86–7
Mushrooms, Ricotta-stuffed with
Sweet Potatoes 17–18

O

Omelette, Sweet Soufflé 93

P

Pancakes
Blueberry 87–8
Chinese 45
Wholemeal Chicken and Ricotta 49
Pasta see also individual headings
Tricolour 16
Peach Melba Meringue Roulade 91
Pear
and Apple Crumble with Custard Sauce 77
Spiced Red Wine Cobbler 81–2
Pea Masala with Sherpa's Pie 68–9
Pronto Penne with Red Pesto 19–20
Pepper and Lamb Kebabs with creamy Haricot Beans 61
Physalis 78, 84
Pizza
with Christmas Coleslaw 13–14
Feasta Meatza 75
Pan-fried Marinara 26–7
Pork Medallions in a Mushroom Sauce 65–6
Potatoes, Fondant 62

R

Raspberries, Star-spangled Soufflés 80–1
Rice
Coconut 22
Egg-fried 54–5
Ricotta
and Wholemeal Chicken Pancakes 49
-stuffed Mushrooms 17

S

Salmon
Blackened Salmon Fillet on Bed of Hot and
Sour Lentils 31
en Croûte 25–6
Rösti with Tartare Sauce 30
Smoked Salmon and Avocado Tagliatelle 28–9
Thai Salmon Fillets with Coconut Rice and Oriental
Vegetables 22
Sausage Sizzlers 58
Sherpa's Pie with Pea Masala 68–9
Soufflés
Cheese with Stilton Sauce and Tomato Bites 14–15
Star-spangled Raspberry 80–1
Strawberry Compote and Baked Alaska 94
Sweet Potatoes 17–18
Sweetcorn Skewers 39
Summer Berry Crisp 92

T

Tabbouleh, with Spiced Fish 33–4
Tacos, Tornado 47
Tarte Tatin and Berry Custard 89
Tiramisu 84–5
Tomato Bites 14–15
Tratziki, with Spiced Lamb 68–9
Trifle, Triple Tipple 88–9
Turkey Golden Cordon Vert 43

V

Vegetables
and Fruit Curry 18–19
Oriental 22
Ribbons 29
Spicy 23